THE OFFICIAL
SIMCITY CLASSIC™
PLANNING COMMISSION
HANDBOOK

THE OFFICIAL SIMCITY CLASSIC™ PLANNING COMMISSION HANDBOOK

Johnny L. Wilson

Osborne **McGraw-Hill**

Berkeley New York St. Louis San Francisco
Auckland Bogotá Hamburg London Madrid
Mexico City Milan Montreal New Delhi Panama City
Paris São Paulo Singapore Sydney
Tokyo Toronto

Osborne **McGraw-Hill**
2600 Tenth Street
Berkeley, California 94710
U.S.A.

For information on translations or book distributors outside of the
U.S.A., please write to Osborne **McGraw-Hill** at the above address.

The Official SimCity Classic™
Planning Commission Handbook

1234567890 DOC 9987654

ISBN 0-07-881998-9

To Susie, Jennifer, and Jonathan, my family

CONTENTS AT A GLANCE

	Why This Book Is for You	1
Chapter 1	The "Sim"ple Joys of Mayorhood	3
Chapter 2	I Love a History: Urban Planning in the Past	39
Chapter 3	The Population Bomb: Human Resources and Problems	55
Chapter 4	Heavy Traffic	65
Chapter 5	Ecology and Entropy	83
Chapter 6	Crash Landing	95
Chapter 7	The Buck Starts Here	111
Chapter 8	Nurture Is Natural	129
Chapter 9	Archives of the Planning Commission	139
Appendix A	Using the Terrain Editor	149
Appendix B	A SimCity Atlas	167
Appendix C	Toys and The Man: An Interview with Will Wright, Inventor of The Software Toy	185
	Bibliography	195
	Index	199

CONTENTS

Foreword | xv
Acknowledgments | xvii
Introduction | xix

Why This Book Is for You | 1

Chapter 1   The "Sim"ple Joys of Mayorhood | 3
Starting from Zero | 3
    Boot Camp: Getting Started | 4
Tools of the Trade | 8
    Moving Heaven and Earth: The
    Bulldozer Icon | 9
    On the Road Again: The Roads
    Icon | 13
    Power to the Power: The Power
    Lines Icon | 14
    Take a Ride on the Railroads:
    The Transit Lines Icon | 15
    Free Parking: The Parks Icon | 15
    Home, Sweet Home: The
    Residential Zones Icon | 16
    A Word from Our Sponsor: The
    Commercial Zones Icon | 20
    Better Living Through Industry:
    The Industrial Zones Icon | 22
    Chips on the Old Block: The
    Police Deparments Icon | 22

Burn, Baby, Burn!: The Fire
    Departments Icon   24
Fourth and Inches: The
    Stadiums Icon   24
Power Pack: The Power Plants
    Icon   25
Down to the Sea in Ships: The
    Sea Ports Icon   26
The Wild Blue Yonder: The
    Airports Icon   26
Goals To Go!: The Purpose of Urban
    Planning   27
PERT—Program Evaluation and
    Review Technique   29
When It Rains, It Pours Department:
    The Disasters Menu   37
What Do the "Sim"ple Folk Do?   38

Chapter 2   **I Love a History: Urban Planning
in the Past**   39
Classical Grasp: Early Cities   40
    Classics Illustrated: Applying
        the Lessons   41
By the Sea: The Role of Ports in
    American Urban History   47
The Tell-Tale Plot: Grid Patterns in
    American Urban Development   49
Zoned In: Efficiency in Urban
    Planning   51
The Green, Green Grass of Home:
    Open Spaces in Urban Planning   51

Chapter 3   **The Population Bomb: Human
Resources and Problems**   55
Up with People: Population Growth
    Projections   56
For the People: Managing Land
    Value   57
    People Who Need People:
        Commercial Considerations   60
    Industrial Strength Planner:
        Industrial Considerations   61

	Urban Jungle: Population Density	62
	Pop! Go the People!: Important Calculations	64
Chapter 4	**Heavy Traffic**	65
	Spontaneous Generation: The Traffic Phenomenon	66
	Give My Regard to Broad Ways: A Wrong Answer	68
	The Haussmann of the Opera: Haussmannization	69
	Uncorking Bottlenecks: A Partial Answer	70
	The SimCity School of Modeling: Traffic Calculations	72
	Not Doing a Slow Bern: Land Use Considerations	75
	Don't Rail on My Parade: Rail Problems	76
	Satellite Development: A Partial Solution	77
	Picking the Public Pocket: Financial Wizardry	80
	Hardening of the Arteries: Conclusions	81
Chapter 5	**Ecology and Entropy**	83
	To Air Is Human: Air Quality	84
	Deadweight in Detroit: Tips on Winning	87
	The Nuclear Option: Energy Choices	89
	The China "Sim"drome: The Boston 2010 Scenario	91
Chapter 6	**Crash Landing**	95
	On the Boardwalk: Seashore and Flood Plain Development	96
	Drain It in Rio: Preventing Floods (Rio de Janeiro)	96
	Whole Lotta' Shakin' Goin' On: Earthquakes	98
	It's Not My Fault: Seismic Zoning	101

	We're All Shook Up: San Francisco	102
	Bomb Voyage: Hamburg	107
	The Monster Is an Ecologist: Tokyo	109
	Crash Course: Air Disasters	110
	Conclusion	110
Chapter 7	**The Buck Starts Here**	**111**
	Where on Earth Is Temecula?	111
	The Wild, Mild West: Historical Summary	112
	What SimCity Doesn't Tell You: Sensitive Areas	114
	What SimCity Doesn't Tell You: Services	119
	Sims in White: Hospital Districts	119
	School Daze: School Districts	121
	Something Rotten in Temecula: Waste Management	122
	Tiled Play: Parks and Recreation	123
	Kilowatt Kraving: Electrical Demand	124
	The "Simecula" Scenario	125
	Conclusions	127
Chapter 8	**Nurture Is Natural**	**129**
	Entropy Is Not the Final Word	130
	Case Study #1	131
	Feedback Is Essential	133
	Case Study #2	133
	Case Study #3	135
	Conclusion	136
Chapter 9	**Archives of the Planning Commission**	**139**
	What's Wrong with This City?	139
	The Airport Blues	140
	Derailing Mass Transit	142
	What's Right About This City?	143
	Never Tampa with Tampa Bay	145
	Final Evaluation	147

Appendix A   **Using the Terrain Editor**   **149**
Let There Be Light: Installing the
   Disks   150
Let the Land Be Separate from the
   Waters: Menus   152
   The Tile Waits on No Land   155
A Tale of Nine Cities   156
   Bad News City   156
   Big City   156
   Deadwood City   158
   Finigan City   158
   Fredsville   161
   Happy, IL   161
   Joffeberg   163
   Linear City   163
   Medieval City   164
And It Was Good   165

Appendix B   **A SimCity Atlas**   **167**
Geometric Cities   167
   Quadripoli   167
   Squaresville   168
   Symmetry City   169
Mirroring Reality   169
   Spikenard, Ohio   170
   Pittsburgh, Pennsylvania   170
Prize Winners   171
   Gilligan City   171
   Tjoseytown   172
Lessons To Be Learned   173

Appendix C   **Toys and The Man: An
Interview with Will Wright,
Inventor of The Software Toy**   **185**

Bibliography   **195**

Index   **199**

FOREWORD

Most of the time I was working on SimCity, I had the feeling that it would attract a rather limited audience of planners, designers, and strategy fans. I never really envisioned the broad appeal—even to people who don't usually play computer games—that it turned out to have. Luckily, my friend and business partner, Jeff Braun, had no such reservations. Looking back on it now, I'm beginning to understand the roots of SimCity's popularity.

When I first started to research city planning, it seemed to me to be an interesting but rather dry, academic subject. As I read more about it, though, I rapidly became fascinated with the different approaches that could be taken. I began to see the city in which I live in a new way, as overlapping layers of zoning decisions, road networks, and power grids. As work on the game progressed, and I started to plan my own simulated cities, I had to face some of the same dilemmas and decisions that arise in real urban planning. At this point, my attraction to the subject grew into an obsession.

What was formerly a dry, static subject to me had now come "alive," as I was able to enter into the planning process. Access to a "toy" city gave me a guinea pig on which I could try out my city planning experiments. Play became a tool for learning. During the development of the program, I was guided by my desire to make sure that other people could experience this interactive discovery of the city planning process.

This is why SimCity ended up with such loosely structured goals. Instead of telling the player how to win or lose, we left it up to the player to decide what the desirable outcome was. A city reflects the values of its designers. Some designers may value aesthetics over functionality. To some, the size of the city may be more important than the happiness of the city's residents. One of the most educational aspects of SimCity occurs when you make decisions about what your ideal city would be. As you begin to build, you begin to realize that visualizing your dream and implementing it are not the same thing.

When I first talked to Johnny Wilson about this book, he described to me how SimCity had inspired him to visit the library and start his own research into urban planning. I knew right away that he was in the program. Reading the drafts for *The SimCity Planning Commission Handbook* has been quite educational and entertaining for me, but also strangely familiar, as I go through the discovery process once again.

Will Wright

ACKNOWLEDGMENTS

Without the help of a great many people, this book would not be possible. I would like to say thanks to Russell Sipe, my employer and partner who taught me how to do what I now do best, write critical analyses of computer games. I would like to express special appreciation to Michael Bremer, a fine writer in his own stead who assisted me with a technical review, screen shots, and additional encouragement. I would like to thank Roger Stewart, Osborne/McGraw-Hill's acquisitions editor for the previous edition of this book, for believing in the project since it was first developed. Finally, I would like to acknowledge the fact that this book would be nothing without the brilliant product created by Will Wright and the business acumen exhibited by Jeff Braun in getting it to market.

INTRODUCTION

The Official SimCity Classic Planning Commission Handbook is designed to be a companion book for those who want to get more out of Maxis Software's SimCity. As a companion book, it is designed to offer background on the game, as well as urban planning in general, and provide insight to help you play the game more effectively. It was written to provide help for the novice SimCity player, useful information for the average SimCity player, and new challenges for the sophisticated player.

Just because it is a companion book to a game doesn't make it a lightweight book, however. Sometimes, when people refer to the previous edition of *The Official SimCity Classic Planning Commission Handbook* as a hint book, I get this irresistible urge to remind them that it is also a college "textbook": it has been used in course work, and as an urban planning resource book by experts in zoning and community safety who have actually contacted me after reading the book. The book's value as a real-life resource combined with the sales success of the original book tell me that I succeeded as an author. I presented enough real-life information to teach readers about urban planning and enough game hints to make their playing more enjoyable. I hope it will do so for you as well.

About This Book

The Official SimCity Classic Planning Commission Handbook attempts to walk you through the start-up process of using the program as though all you have is a SimCity disk and a computer. Throughout this book we use the term "SimCity" to refer to both the original SimCity and the SimCity Classic versions.

Even if you have never played a computer game before, you should be able to follow the step-by-step instructions in order to get the program installed and running. Even if you may have never thought about city planning until now, you should be able to learn many of the concepts that drive the growth of modern urban communities. Even if you have never been able to "build" anything before, SimCity gives you the chance to build the environment of your dreams. The goal of *The Official SimCity Classic Planning Commission Handbook* is to smooth the rough edges and help you create that environment with less frustration than you would experience in trying to solve certain problems on your own.

How This Book Is Organized

The Official SimCity Classic Planning Commission Handbook is divided into nine chapters and three appendixes. Chapter 1 is designed to lead the novice player through the basic mechanics of the game and identify some of the problems and misconceptions that new players often have about how the SimCity model works. Chapter 2 is designed to inform all players about the history of urban development and how playing SimCity usually differs from the historical development of cities. It offers a challenge for those who are willing to use SimCity to re-create a historical city. Chapter 3 talks about the population equation, the ticking time bomb that affects both "Sim" cities and real cities. It offers some ideas for handling population-related problems. Chapter 4 deals with the most realistic aspect of SimCity, the traffic model. The game not only discusses the reality of traffic problems, but suggests ways to solve traffic problems in playing SimCity and, in particular, winning the Bern, Switzerland scenario.

Chapter 5 discusses two particular types of pollution: air pollution and nuclear radiation. In addition to a brief discussion of these two major problems, the chapter focuses on ways to win at the Detroit (recession) scenario and Boston (nuclear meltdown) scenario. Chapter 6 raises the ante in terms of problem solving. This chapter offers background on dealing with air, sea, flood, earthquake, and supernatural disasters. Readers will discover how to cope with the San Francisco (1906) earthquake; a future flood in Rio de Janeiro; the World War II bombing of Hamburg, Germany; and Tokyo visited by a gigantic lizard (who says everything has to be reality-based to be fun?).

With Chapter 7 the pace of the book changes somewhat. In this chapter, I examine a recently incorporated area in Southern California and discuss the stress of development, necessity of planning, tension between developer greed and quality of life, and parallels with the SimCity model. A difficult scenario for readers to attempt is presented. Following on the heels of the seventh chapter, Chapter 8 offers a few sage words of advice for those who simply want to refine and polish their city models. This chapter takes something of an "organic" look at the makeup of both real and "Sim" cities. Finally, Chapter 9 offers an annotated catalog of potential mistakes. Glancing through the screen shots and notes about different authors' poor designs and errors can be a useful experience in itself.

Appendix A follows much the same procedure as Chapter 1, except that its subject is an ancillary product called the SimCity Terrain Editor. Designed for the novice player, the appendix tells how to install the editor and offers simple instructions for using it. It even shares instructions on using the editor to "cheat" on established "Sim" cities. The appendix ends with annotations on nine city files included on the Terrain Editor disks. Appendix B uses the same basic annotation formula to critique cities that were entered in a contest sponsored by Maxis Software. Appendix C, new to this edition, is an interview with SimCity's designer, Will Wright.

A bibliography of works cited is included for those of you who might want to pursue the subject of urban planning more extensively.

Conventions Used in This Book

In *The Official SimCity Classic Planning Commission Handbook*, you will notice several commands which instruct you to type a particular word and press the ENTER key. You should type the words exactly as printed in CAPS prior to pressing the ENTER key. In this way, you can be certain of exactly what to type when dealing with DOS commands.

Every possible attempt has been made to reproduce SimCity screens in this book by using actual screenshots. However, some figures were reproduced from printed maps and diagrams because the original files were unavailable. These figures will not have the same definition as most of the art in this book.

Why This Book Has Been Written

SimCity has a phenomenal appeal far beyond most computer games. The reasons for this appeal are undoubtedly as varied as the thousands of people who have purchased the game. Some like the idea of playing a game where they can establish their own rules; others like the program's similarity to an erector set, where their creation can "come to life" and amaze even the creators. Still others like the idea of a program that realistically models the complex systems of urban life and offers a chance to solve some of those problems; a few simply enjoy building a functioning city on their computer and dismantling it with any number of natural disasters.

Another reason for the popularity of SimCity may be the fact that it is more of a *toy* than a *game*. By toy, of course, I mean that the program is not as competitive as those computer and/or board games where players try to defeat each other or the artificial opponent programmed into the software. Instead, SimCity can be as open-ended and non-competitive as the player wishes it to be. It offers opportunities for no-risk experiments and a chance for many of us who are not artistic to allow our creativity to flow out in simulated urban designs. Unlike many games, when you play SimCity, you do not have your ego on the line. Instead, you have the opportunity to envision the perfect environment, plan for this environment to take shape, and watch what will actually happen.

After numerous playing sessions with SimCity, I am convinced that SimCity players begin with an ethereal vision of the ultimate city design and end up with cities that approximate that dream, yet are peppered with the warts of urban realities. So, much of the joy to be found in the program is tied up in the cosmetic surgery necessary to remove these blemishes of metropolitan life.

Depending on your point of view, it can be either unfortunate or quite fortunate that there are no hard and fast rules for solving the problems posed by SimCity. This is unfortunate because the dearth of answers suggests that our society is still a long way from finding the solutions to many of our urban ills. For the gamer, this is fortunate because it means that there are numerous ways to play the game and many different kinds of experiments to try in seeking the optional solutions.

Whatever the reasons for SimCity's popularity, it has cut a wide swath through the awards process for computer game products. After winning a host of magazine awards (including the 1989 Game of the Year from *Computer Gaming World* magazine), the game managed to net four major awards from the Software Publishers Association (equivalent to a major sweep at the Academy Awards).

In addition to its success as a game, SimCity has had a major impact on education. I was particularly impressed with the Future City Competition, sponsored by 15 engineering societies and led by the Institute of Electrical and Electronics Engineers (IEEE) and Chevron. Held in early 1993, more than 200 middle schools and junior high schools participated in the contest and all were provided with copies of SimCity donated by Maxis. The goal of the contest was to design a people-oriented, environmentally sound city for the 21st century which would be both energy and cost efficient.

Tilden Middle School of Rockville, Maryland won this year's contest and received a $1,000 grant for its math and science programs and an IBM laptop. In the photo in Figure I-1, Matthew Smith shows a printout of the Tilden Town map to President Clinton. The foreground shows a model of Tilden Town which the students constructed from the SimCity map.

Not only has the game been used for model city contests, it has been used in college classrooms as well. SimCity provides a fresh way of viewing urban problems and, because of its relative simplicity and ability to relate models to each other, sometimes helps planners see potential problems before they develop. Since cities provide a space for uniting disparate individuals, races, and cultures into a viable whole, the game has a tremendous socializing capacity, just from having different players examine their different approaches to city building.

Figure I-1. President Clinton at the Future Cities Competition

A Brief History of SimCity

Will Wright, the "really cool dude" who wrote SimCity, started work on the game in late 1984 or early 1985. He had already created the commercially successful Raid On Bungling Bay for Broderbund Software and was ready for a new challenge. Raid On Bungling Bay was an arcade game in which you flew a bomber over various types of terrain and tried to take out the right kinds of targets.

Upon completing Raid, Wright found himself tentatively writing a game that involved robots and utilized three basic shapes (squares, triangles, and circles). Will and his friends jokingly referred to this game as an Electronic Arts Construction Set, since it used the three shapes found in the rival company's logo; the rival company was known, in early years, for construction sets (programs that enabled you to design your own games).

Somehow, however, the game just wasn't coming together and Will found himself continually returning to a familiar piece of code. It seems that Will had created a tile editor in order to develop city/industry/target scenery for Raid On Bungling Bay, and he found that he just couldn't stop returning to the tile editor and creating cities. He says that creating the cities was something like building the dioramas of military scenes that he had enjoyed in his boyhood.

Then, several events occurred that had a profound influence on Will Wright and the history of SimCity. First, Will was showing his neighbor, Bruce Joffe, what his tile editor could do. He wanted Joffe's opinion about how realistic certain model cities, which he had created with the tile editor, actually looked. Joffe was just the right person to ask. He had studied under Dr. Jay Forester at MIT. Dr. Forester was a pioneer in dynamic modeling of urban environments from the 1950s onward. In those days, Forester was building three-dimensional models on tabletops and physically changing the models after receiving statistical updates from the computer center. Joffe readily saw the potential for adapting the tile editor into a dynamic urban model, so he started loaning books on urban planning to Will.

At the same time, Will reread a unique collection of short stories by Stanislaw Lem. This anthology, *The Cyberiad*, largely recounts the escapades and misadventures of the two greatest constructors in the universe, Trurl and Klapaucius. These great constructors (inventors) could create anything.

In one of these adventures, Trurl comes across a deposed tyrant, Excelsius by name, who had been exiled because of his oppressive ways. Excelsius begged Trurl to construct an invention that would restore him to his place as ruler, but Trurl was not about to enslave anew the citizens of Excelsius' former planetary system. Instead, Trurl created a kingdom in a box for the tyrant. With this invention, Excelsius could fight wars, collect taxes, demand tribute, order executions, enact legislation, and more. When Excelsius saw how well the system worked, he became immersed in his kingdom in the box. Later, the citizens in the box united and overthrew Excelsius.

After rereading this story and talking to Bruce Joffe, the idea for SimCity began to crystallize. He decided that it would be really neat for the city to come to life and for the terrain to undergo change as the city grew.

There was another tie-in with the Lem story, however. Just as Excelsius had enjoyed oppressing his simulated citizens, Will noticed that whenever he demonstrated the game, people would build up a city to a certain point, and then become manic with the Bulldozer icon. People seemed to have as much fun tearing down their cities as they did building them up. So, Will decided to put disasters in the game to allow players the option of calling out disasters and wreaking havoc on their cities.

It is entirely possible that SimCity would have been published in 1986, except for the last event that occurred that influenced its development: Will's wife, Joell, gave birth to their precious daughter. Will took off nearly the entire year to be with his daughter. Then, when he finished the basic game, he could not get it published.

Will went to Broderbund to get SimCity published, but the acquisitions department there did not believe there was enough "game" to the product. They urged Will to put in some scenarios. Nevertheless, the C-64/128 version of SimCity on sale today is essentially the same as the one that could not be published in 1987.

With the C-64/128 game sitting on the shelf, Will eventually programmed a new and more complex SimCity on the Macintosh, formed a new software publishing firm called Maxis Software (with Jeff Braun), and got ready for his initial rave review in *Computer Gaming World*, followed by dozens more. Even *Newsweek* magazine and "ABC News" noticed this small software company with the fascinating product.

More conversions of the program followed and, as of the writing of this book, Maxis stands poised at the threshold of releasing three equally unique products. From little things such as tile editors, knowledgeable neighbors, and clever science fiction stories, arose an amazing program.

How to Use This Book

If you are a complete novice to SimCity or have limited experience with the game, you will want to begin with the first chapter and read the book straight through. If you have a modicum of experience with SimCity, you may want to pick and choose the order in which you read the information. Find the subject that interests you in the table of contents or index and follow it through the book. Then, do the same with another subject. If you are an advanced SimCity player, you may want to try the challenge of building a city from the seaport out (found in the second chapter) or immediately plunge into the Simecula scenario (found in Chapter 7).

No matter what level player you consider yourself to be, every chapter of *The Official SimCity Classic Planning Commission Handbook* is intended to be useful and, hopefully, entertaining. Now, it's up to you, Mr. or Ms. Mayor.

WHY THIS BOOK IS FOR YOU

Since there are no hard and fast answers to the challenges faced in SimCity, many of you are wondering why you should read any further in *The Official SimCity Classic Planning Commission Handbook*. This handbook is not intended to tell you precisely how to play every aspect of the game. Instead, it is intended to complement your playing experience by offering insights into the realities behind the program, some of the ways the program resolves certain problems, why the design does what it does, and how to improve your score. In addition, *The Official SimCity Classic Planning Commission Handbook* is intended to serve as something like a laboratory workbook. It offers several experiments that you can try and a challenging scenario based on an actual community undergoing rapid development. It is hoped that this book will stimulate, challenge, and inform you about SimCity in particular, and about city planning in general.

CHAPTER 1
THE "SIM"PLE JOYS OF MAYORHOOD

This one's for all of you who've ever thrown down your morning newspaper in disgust after reading that your local planning commission has just approved a commercial development expected to increase traffic along an already congested road. It's also for all of you who've grimaced with a migraine headache after hearing your city council vote down that much-needed stoplight. It's especially for all of you who think you could do better.

Starting from Zero

When Walter Gropius founded the Bauhaus commune (officially *Staatliches Bauhaus*) in post-World War I Germany (1919), he possessed a strong conviction that blending the arts and architecture into a unity, while searching for the "clean and pure" in form and structure, would bring about a social revolution leading toward an urban utopia. Against the rubble of postwar Europe, the idea of "starting from zero" came to epitomize the revolutionary changes that these artists and architects were trying to implement.

SimCity and SimCity Classic offer you a fast and efficient perspective from which to view the basics of urban planning. They allow you to draw a unique city plan on a blank canvas (a map, 10 miles by 10 miles, representing 100 square miles of undeveloped land) and to solve realistic problems faced by leaders of actual, historical cities. This chapter will familiarize you with the tools available in SimCity; it will describe the goals of urban planning in general (while explaining how SimCity relates these goals to your score); and it will provide scenarios to test these approaches using SimCity. If you are already familiar with the editing tools in SimCity, you'll want to skip directly to the section of this chapter entitled "Goals to Go!: The Purpose of Urban Planning".

Note: Whenever we refer to SimCity in this book we're referring to both the original SimCity and SimCity Classic, except when it comes to the specific installation instructions that you'll find below.

Boot Camp: Getting Started

This section is designed to help you get started if you have not yet played SimCity. Since this section is machine and game specific, you should skip to the section related to the computer or version of the game that you will be using.

Amiga   SimCity, as opposed to SimCity Classic, was available on the Amiga. If you own SimCity and you're an Amiga user, you should know that two versions of SimCity were available: one requiring one megabyte of RAM and one requiring only 512K. If you have an older version of SimCity Amiga and would like the "downgrade" to the 512K version, you should contact Maxis Software directly.

Amiga users may wish to install SimCity on a hard disk. If you are playing from the production copy, you will also want to create a "Save Game" disk on which to save you city files.

Now you are ready to boot your Amiga and either insert the SimCity disk or start the program from the hard drive. Users who have complex computer systems that use a lot of RAM may find that they are having problems running SimCity when they do not start from the production disk. Therefore, we recommend booting the program from the production disk. Then, when the SimCity disk icon appears, double-click on it. When the SimCity program icon appears, double-click on that icon and the main title screen will appear as shown in Figure 1-1. Now you're ready to skip to the section entitled "Tools of the Trade."

Atari ST   If you own the original SimCity and are using an Atari ST, you should boot the computer from the SimCity production disk. Then, when the SimCity disk icon appears, double-click on it. When the SimCity program icon appears, double-click on the icon and the main title screen will appear as shown in Figure 1-1. Now you're ready to skip to the section entitled "Tools of the Trade."

C-64/128   If you are using a C-64/128 (a joystick is required) and you own the original SimCity, you will want to be able to save your city data. This means that you will need to create a special data disk before booting the program. To create a data disk, turn on your computer and place a new disk into your drive. Type

OPEN 15,8,15,"NO:CITY DISK 1,C1

and press ENTER. Later, you can create new data disks (CITY DISK 2, for example). Now you are ready to place the SimCity program disk in the drive and type **LOAD"SC",8,1**. Press ENTER and SimCity will load. Now you can skip to the section entitled "Tools of the Trade."

Figure 1-1. The main title screen

IBM   Installation instructions for SimCity and SimCity Classic are a bit different. See your user's manual and read the sections below before installing.

If you are using the original SimCity IBM version, you will want to install SimCity either on two floppy disks or on your hard disk before reading further. (Actually, you can install SimCity on one floppy disk, but should you install a high-resolution color graphics set to a floppy disk that can only hold 360K, you will have no room for the built-in scenarios on that disk. You will have to use DOS commands to copy those files onto your Save Game disk.) Whether you are playing from the production disk or from an installed floppy, you will also need to format a disk on which to save your city files.

To install SimCity, you simply boot your computer and, if you are not booting from the floppy drive, change to the floppy drive. At the prompt (usually A >), type **INSTALL** and press ENTER. The screen will display the following question: "Install from drive: [*] A:, [ ] B:." Use the RIGHTARROW or LEFTARROW key on the keypad to move the asterisk to the drive from which you will be copying SimCity. Then press ENTER and the program will ask you to confirm the drive. Naturally, typing an **N** will allow you to back up and correct the mistake, while typing **Y** will continue the installation procedure. Next, you will be asked "Install from drive: [ ] A:, [ ] B:, [*] C:, [ ] D:." You will be able to move the asterisk in the same way you did earlier, indicating which drive contains the disk onto which you wish to copy SimCity. If you are installing to a hard disk, the prompt will read "Destination Directory -> C:\SIMCITY" (or "D:\SIMCITY" if that is the correct designation). If you are installing to a floppy disk, the prompt will read, "   -> B:\" (or "A:\" if that is the correct drive).

Warning: Many people who have used the Install program to copy SimCity to separate floppy disks were not previously aware of the use of subdirectories (used to divide hard disks into smaller, more accessible sections), so they either typed in a subdirectory name or typed **Y** when the Install program asked if they wanted to install SimCity to a subdirectory. Then, when they were ready to run the program, they couldn't find it. This problem can be avoided by simply pressing ENTER at that point in the Install program. When you press ENTER, you will be asked for confirmation, just as you were earlier.

Once you have completed this process, you will be asked to select and confirm the right graphics display for your system. There are three high-resolution monochrome graphics sets (Hercules, CGA, and EGA, which have, respectively, 720 x 348, 640 x 200, and 640 x 350 pixel resolutions). CGA owners should note that they will not see colors on the screen, nor will EGA owners who only have 128K of video RAM or 512K of system RAM, but want high resolution. Tandy owners will get 16 colors in low resolution (320 x 200) with only 128K video RAM or 512K system RAM and 640K system RAM. An MCGA version is also available as an upgrade.

Next, you may select a JOYSTICK, if desired, and select the sound option.

You are finally ready to use SimCity. Now either change your hard disk directory to the SIMCITY directory or place your installed floppy in drive A or B. Then type **SIMCITY** at the appropriate prompt (A>, B>, C>, or D>) and the main title screen will appear as shown in Figure 1-1. Now skip to the section entitled "Tools of the Trade."

If you are installing SimCity Classic on an IBM PC or compatible, you'll find that installation is very simple. Boot up your computer and put your disk labeled Disk 1 in either your A or B floppy drive. Now type **A:** or **B:** and press ENTER, depending upon which drive you put the disk in. At the prompt on your screen, type **INSTALL** and press ENTER and follow the installation instructions on your screen.

Macintosh If you're a Macintosh user installing SimCity, you will want to create a formatted disk for the purpose of saving your city files. Then you simply boot your computer and insert your SimCity disk. If you are using a machine with only 512K of RAM, you should boot from the production disk because it has a very skimpy system file that allows the program to run in the available RAM. Then double-click on the SimCity icon and you will be presented with the initial options. Now skip to the section entitled "Tools of the Trade."

To install SimCity Classic and the Terrain Editor to your hard disk, first make a new folder called SimCity. There are both color and monochrome versions of SimCity Classic for the Mac. To install color SimCity, drag the contents of both disks, except version 1.4, into the folder on your hard disk. To install the monochrome version of SimCity, drag the contents of both disks, except version 1.4c, into the folder on your hard disk.

Note: Be sure that the Scenario File and the program files are in the same folder.

The file Cities.sea on Disk 2 is a self-extracting archive containing several cities. If you would like these cities on your hard disk so that you will be able to play with them, select the Cities.sea folder on your hard disk and then click on EXTRACT.

Note: When playing Monochrome SimCity on a color or grey-scale monitor, set it to black and white two-color mode in the Control Panel.

You will find complete instructions for using the Terrain Editor to custom design terrains at the end of your SimCity Classic manual.

Super Nintendo If you are playing SimCity on the Super Nintendo Entertainment System (SNES), please insert the cartridge into the standard slot and power up the system. You are now ready to learn the "Tools of the Trade."

Tools of the Trade

First of all, on all the machines except for the C-64/128, you will be given the following choices:

- Start A New City
- Load A City
- Select A Scenario

On the Commodore, you start with new terrain and must select the Disk Access menu in order to load a city (whether it is a prefabricated city for a scenario or one that you have previously saved). At this point (unless you are playing on the C-64/128 or NES), the program will ask you what difficulty level you wish play (Easy, Medium, or Hard).

Next, you'll want to know how to navigate about the map. The scrolling is slightly different on each machine format.

IBM On the IBM-PC and compatibles, you simply move the arrow (cursor) in the direction you want the map to scroll. Once the cursor itself reaches the edge of the screen, scrolling begins.

Macintosh   On the Macintosh and Amiga versions, you move from a macroscopic (big picture) view of the map to a smaller working perspective by positioning a movable window (cursor) on the area of the larger map that you want to work with. On the Macintosh, you simply double-click on that rectangle and the program zooms in to the proper perspective for inputting your decisions (called the Close-Up Map in the SimCity documentation). On the Macintosh, interestingly enough, one can scroll the map by using the standard Macintosh window boxes, but there is also a special Joystick box in the upper right-hand corner of the Macintosh window. It is divided into nine smaller squares, corresponding roughly to nine areas of the larger screen. When you point and click on one of these areas, the entire screen scrolls, bringing the corresponding area of the larger screen into view.

Amiga   On the Amiga, you select the area with the rectangular cursor, and then click on the Return to Editor button in the lower right-hand corner of the map or graph screen to get to the working perspective.

Note: Newer IBM versions also utilize the Macintosh click and drag function to move the rectangle around the map.

C-64/128   On the C-64/128, you must plug your joystick into Port #2. You start by moving a window (cursor) around the map screen (the big picture) until you find the section of terrain you want to edit. Then you use the arrow keys to highlight the Close-Up Map icon pictured on the on-screen control panel (under the map itself). If you press ENTER while this icon is lit, the screen will zoom in and display the Close-Up Map where the real game occurs.

Now let's look at the screen, as pictured in Figure 1-2. The top of the screen should be relatively easy to understand. A *message bar* displays your available funds, the city's name in the current simulation, and the current date (in game time). At various points during the simulation, you will receive prompts on the right-hand side of this message bar, which will tell you when more roads, residential zones, commercial zones, power plants, and so on are needed, or when your "Sims" are demanding an airport, stadium, fire department, police department, or whatever. It is absolutely vital to pay attention to these messages if you want to keep your score up and your city progressing.

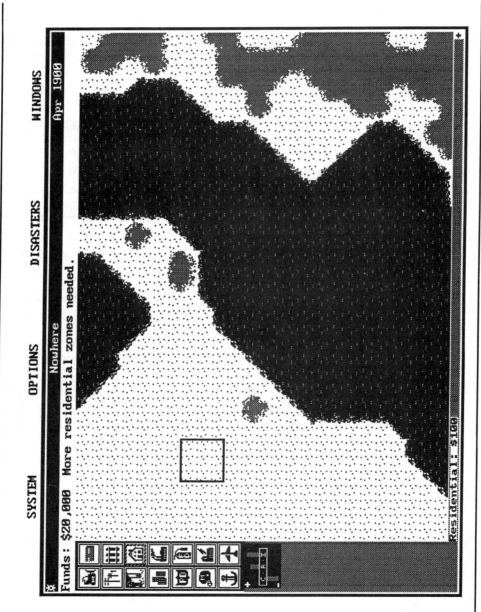

Figure 1-2. The basic SimCity screen (IBM pictured)

On the left-hand side of the Close-Up Map (on the IBM) are the *icons*, which are shown in Figure 1-3. These represent the tools you will use to sculpt your city out of nothingness (when you are "starting from zero") or to perform surgery on urban problems when you are managing one of the "historical" scenarios. Note that these icons are located on the right side of the Amiga Edit Window, lined up underneath the C-64/128 Edit Window, aligned along the left edge on the Macintosh (but not in the same order as on the IBM), and positioned on the left on the NES. For consistency, the icons will be described in the order in which they are found on the IBM and compatibles.

 Moving Heaven and Earth: The Bulldozer Icon

The top left corner contains the Bulldozer icon. This tool simulates excavation and earth-moving work preparatory to any actual construction. Perform the following steps in order to learn to use the tool.

1. Move the arrow (cursor) until it points at the Bulldozer icon.

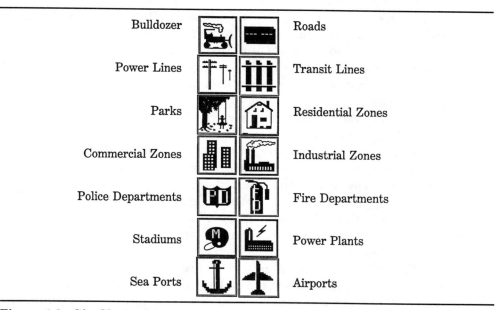

Figure 1-3. SimCity tool icons

2. Press the SPACEBAR, joystick, or left mouse button on the IBM, the left mouse button on the Amiga, the mouse button on the Macintosh, or the fire button on the Nintendo.

Note: No matter what icon is selected in the Amiga and IBM versions, pressing the right mouse button activates the Bulldozer. Press the left mouse button for all other functions.

3. Move the arrow back onto the Close-Up Map. Notice that the cursor has turned into a small square.

4. Position the square over some of the wooded terrain on the map.

5. Click the button or press the SPACEBAR again and you will have clear terrain in the exact shape of that square.

6. Repeat the process and it will work as often as you like, until you choose another icon. Note, however, that if you are bulldozing a residential, commercial, or industrial zone and click on the exact center of that zone, you will automatically destroy everything in that zone.

On the C-64/128, you will use the following procedure for all the editing tools to be discussed, including the Bulldozer icon. C-64/128 owners will use the cursor keys to highlight the proper icon (located beneath the Close-Up Map), and then utilize the joystick to scroll the terrain under the pointer until it is located over the spot to be edited. Then you simply press the joystick button, and the change takes place on the map.

If you haven't played SimCity prior to reading this book, it may be a good idea to play with this tool right now. For instance, scroll around the map until you find some heavily wooded terrain. Click on the Bulldozer icon and move the cursor box to the wooded terrain. Since we won't be saving this city, you can do something "off the wall" just to make sure you understand how the bulldozing function works. Position the cursor box in the wooded area and start clicking so that you print one of your initials in the terrain. If you can do this, you have the function locked.

The good news is that, unless you are playing on the C-64/128, you may not have to bulldoze every small square area. On all formats except the C-64/128, the program starts in a default mode called Auto-Bulldoze. With this function selected, you will not have to bulldoze prior to zoning for residential, commercial, or industrial development (the excavation costs are automatically assumed), and you do not have to bulldoze prior to building roads or railroads.

"Why then," you may well ask, "did we learn how to use this icon?" The Bulldozer icon in important for fine-tuning the terrain along the way and for use in restricting growth. For fine-tuning, there will be times when you need to bulldoze a bit of coastline in order to fit a residential zone right next to the water. If you're just getting acquainted with SimCity, you might want to try positioning the cursor box on part of the shoreline and clicking on it. Notice how it squares off the uneven edges with landfill so that the corner of a new development zone can be wedged in. For restricting growth, you may decide that you don't want a residential area to grow any larger (think of it as an anti-condo ordinance). Rather than wiping out the entire residential zone and starting over, you simply bulldoze one corner of the zone and plant a park (see the section entitled, "Free Parking: The Parks Icon"). This freezes the zone at its current level of development.

The costs of using the Bulldozer icon are straightforward. It costs $1 for each small section of land that is bulldozed.

 ## On the Road Again: The Roads Icon

Move the cursor box all the way to the left so that it scrolls off the Close-Up Map and becomes an arrow cursor again. Point the arrow to the box immediately to the right of the Bulldozer icon and click (following the instructions noted previously in the section on the Bulldozer icon) on the Roads icon. Then move the arrow back onto the Close-Up Map so that it becomes a cursor box. Now, wherever you click, a small section of road will appear. There is a slight complication, however. Road sections connect together. Set the box in the middle of some clear terrain and click. You should have a section of road resting horizontally in an east-west orientation (see Figure 1-4). Now, move the cursor box directly north of the road section on the map, keeping the box right next to the original road section. When you click this time, the sections should join together to form a longer section resting vertically in a north-south orientation.

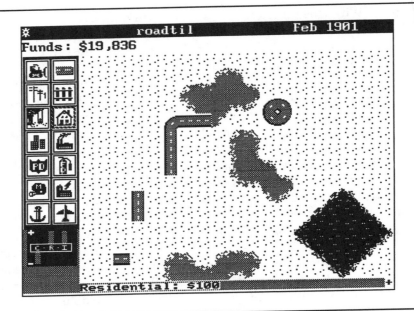

Figure 1-4. Various road patterns

Now the procedure gets a little more interesting. If you place the cursor box at a right angle to the east of the northernmost road section, you will get a section of road that curves to the right when you click your button or press the SPACEBAR. If you keep moving and clicking in a circular motion, you will get an oval similar to a traffic circle. Find a clear space on the map and try to write one of your initials in script to prove that you've mastered the use of this tool.

Note also that you can build roads over water and the program will automatically build bridges for you. You cannot, however, change directions to build circular, S-curve, or T-intersection bridges. The economics of building roads are a little more complex that the costs of leveling a square of land. Therefore, it pays to build sparingly across bodies of water. It costs $10 to build a section of road and $50 to construct one section of a bridge. In addition, the transportation department asks for annual funding of $1 per section of road and $4 per section of bridge in order to maintain this portion of the infrastructure.

Power to the People: The Power Lines Icon

Directly under the Bulldozer icon is the Power Lines icon. You may access it in the same way you accessed the Bulldozer and Roads icons. You can build power lines in exactly the same way that you can build roads, but the turns will appear as right angles rather than curves. Try constructing a rectangle made from power lines in order to demonstrate that you have mastered the use of this tool.

Just as you can build bridges over bodies of water with the roads, you can place "underwater" cables to carry power across the water. You cannot change directions with cables, so be certain that you can get straight to where you're going before you start laying cable.

Again, the costs of building lines across water constrain you to be careful. Where it only costs $5 to construct land-based power lines, $25 per section is required to lay underwater cable. Further, you should be as efficient as possible in planning the power grid, because power lines lose some power due to inefficiencies in transmission. Be certain, therefore, that your power grid is as efficient as you can possibly make it, but be sure to duplicate some lines so that a small disaster doesn't black out the entire city.

 ## Take a Ride on the Railroads: The Transit Lines Icon

Immediately underneath the Roads icon and adjacent to the Power Lines icon, you will find the Transit Lines icon. Perhaps the most obvious bias in the SimCity model is the built-in preference for mass transit. The tool works in exactly the same way as the Roads icon, except that transit lines that traverse bodies of water are treated as tunnels rather than bridges. The advantage of mass transit consists in the capacity to reduce high-density traffic areas and pollution. The disadvantage of mass transit lies strictly in its higher construction ($20 for construction of each normal section of track and $100 for each tunnel section) and maintenance costs ($4 for each normal section and $10 for each section of tunnel).

Note that the C-64/128 version of the game does not have the Transit Lines icon. It derives from an earlier version and has a Waterways icon instead. These man-made streams add to land values, just like parks, because they add to the Quality of Life factor in the game. They aid in slowing fires down, but will not extinguish a fire as a fire break would.

Free Parking: The Parks Icon

Directly underneath the Power Lines icon, you will find the Parks icon. When you click on this tool, you will get a small square equivalent in size to those made by the Bulldozer icon. When you place the square over a clear piece of terrain and click you mouse button or press the SPACEBAR, a park is established. The park squares constructed by using this editing tool appear in some variety. Some of the *terrain tiles* that appear on your city map are all green (representing the vegetation in the park), but some of the tiles will have animated fountains on them.

One novice SimCity player left a franite message on a computer network asking if anyone knew why his parks occasionally had little squares with all sorts of dots moving around. As could be expected, he received several flippant answers to his query. One fellow answered rather candidly that the square was a fountain, adding a humorous afterthought that this must be where "Sim birds" bathe. Another scribe observed that he thought these squares were "Sim doggie pooh" and indicative of the lack of a leash law in his city.

Regardless of what the novice mayor thought these animated dots were, the park squares are important. Planting planned open spaces (parks) enhances the land value of adjacent zones, which in turn reduces the tendency toward crime. Parks prevent overbuilding in residential zones, reserve space for later expansion, and act as fire breaks around zones.

The economics of establishing parks are relatively simple. It costs $10 per park square. To familiarize yourself with this editing tool, try this exercise.

1. Select the Bulldozer icon and clear a section of terrain into a rectangle that is six squares high by six squares wide.

2. Select the Parks icon and place the cursor box in the upper left-hand corner of the newly bulldozed area.

3. Click the mouse button or press the SPACEBAR to establish a park in that corner.

4. Move the cursor box one step below and one step to the right and click again. Then, move the cursor box one step to the right and one step up. Click again. Continue the procedure until you fill the entire rectangle with a checkerboard of park square, clear square, park square, and so forth (see Figure 1-5).

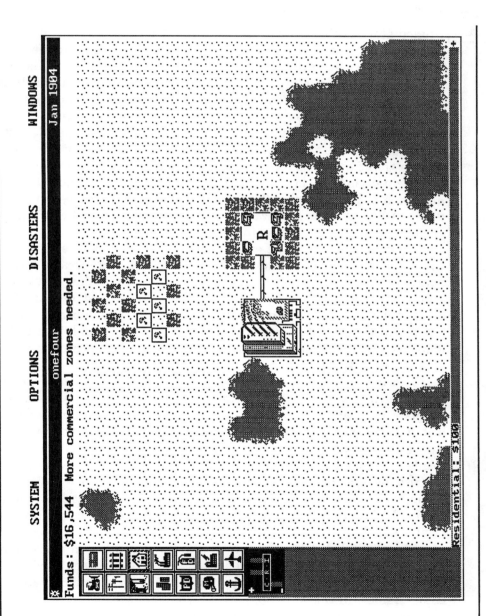

Figure 1-5. Checkerboards and fire breaks

Home, Sweet Home: The Residential Zones Icon

Immediately to the right of the Parks icon on the Icon menu is the Residential Zones icon. When you select this tool and move to the map, you'll notice a significant change. Now when the arrow cursor changes into a cursor box, the area covered is significantly larger than those areas affected by the icons discussed previously. Once you place the cursor box over a section of terrain and click the mouse button or press the SPACEBAR, you get a plot of land zoned for residential use. It costs a flat $100 to zone each residential plot, and there is no maintenance cost to the city. The plots of land zoned as residential are initially represented as clear boxes, but they slowly evolve through different animated terrain tiles to reflect growth, population density, and later, decay. After the homes are connected to the power grid, the evolution of these residential zones begins.

First, the zones consist entirely of single-family homes. Then, as the town grows larger, there is a transition to larger and larger apartment houses (or condominiums). Some residential zones will appear as churches and hospitals as well. This is not because the designers wanted to convert the players or to create tax-exempt zones, but because these are the most recognizable public buildings to be found in any residential neighborhood. Schools and government buildings would look too much like commercial buildings.

This brings up another SimCity anecdote. Many people have called *Computer Gaming World*'s editorial offices, as well as Maxis' customer support lines, wanting to know the formula by which churches and hospitals appear in the residential zones, and whether they reduced the city's overall tax base. There is a basic one-in-ten chance of a residential zone becoming a church or hospital during the early years of a city, but as population density increases, it drops to one-in-fifteen. Their presence does not decrease the tax base, but because many players believe that it does, they have a tendency to bulldoze churches right and left.

Maxis decided that this state of affairs was rather impious, and since natural disasters are referred to as "Acts of God" in legal parlance, they decided to literalize the term in the IBM version (and only in the IBM version). In this version, players who bulldoze churches are apt to bring a tornado upon the city. Nevertheless, one SimCity mayor wrote us that he considered bulldozing churches to be a "blasphemy."

Then, he irreverently added (with apologies to Groucho Marx), "Is it a blast for you, too?" Hopefully, the heretical mayor was a Macintosh user!

Since you really cannot visualize how the Residential Zones icon works until the zone is connected to power, you may want to skip to the "Power Pack" section of this chapter before proceeding. Once you have constructed the power plant, you will be able to continue.

Build a power plant (either coal or nuclear) and return to the Icon menu. Click on the Residential Zones icon and return to the map. Position the cursor box over an area you would like to be a residential neighborhood and click the mouse button or press the SPACEBAR. Note that the newly zoned lot is flashing with a lightning symbol in the center as shown here.

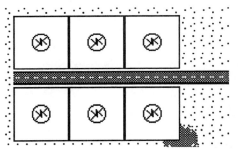

This means that the neighborhood is not yet function. Return to the Icon menu. Select the Power Lines icon. Return to the map and construct a line from the power plant to the residential neighborhood. After this is connected, it should only be a minute or so until the flashing lightning symbol disappears and another couple of minutes until houses start appearing as shown here.

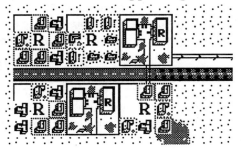

(Of course, they won't stay long unless the "Sims" who live there have a place to work and a way to get there.)

If you have accomplished this, you might want to return to the Icon menu and click on the Parks icon. Then, if you return to the map and plant park squares all around the exterior of the neighborhood, you will have a fire break like the one in Figure 1-5.

A Word from Our Sponsor: The Commercial Zones Icon

On the Icon menu, the icon placed immediately under the Parks icon is the Commercial Zones icon. This icon is the tool for zoning a plot of land as a commercial zone. It works like the Residential Zones icon and costs the same $100 per plot to establish the zone. Like the terrain tiles that represent buildings in the residential zones, the terrain tiles in these zones also evolve. The zones begin with small retail stores, gas stations, and strip centers, and later metamorphose into high-rise office buildings and parking garages.

If you have already built a power plant and established a residential zone, it is a simple matter to create a commercial development. Simply select the Commercial Zones icon and place the cursor box over some clear terrain. Then click on the mouse button or press the SPACEBAR so that the flashing square is place on the map. Connect a power line to the plant and you're almost finished. Because a commercial development has to have customers in order to survive, however, you must construct either a road or a mass transit line from the residential zone to the new development in order for it to succeed.

There is one mistake that novice players often make in constructing this first access road. They usually have the road or rail line "dead end" into both the commercial and residential plots (so that the border of the zone "crosses the T" of the road or rail line). This is not only unnecessary—it is inefficient. It is enough to construct the road or rail line along at least one outside edge of the zone you wish to service.

You can test the model behind the game by creating two different commercial zones, but not connecting the power lines until the last minute. For one commercial zone, establish residential zones on each side and construct roads adjacent to all four sides of the zone. For the other, create two residential zones and place only one road connecting these residential zones to the commercial zones. Then connect the commercial zones to power as closely to the exact same time as possible. Notice which zone grows fastest. As you would except, the one with the greatest traffic density and best residential access is the one that blossoms first (see Figure 1-6).

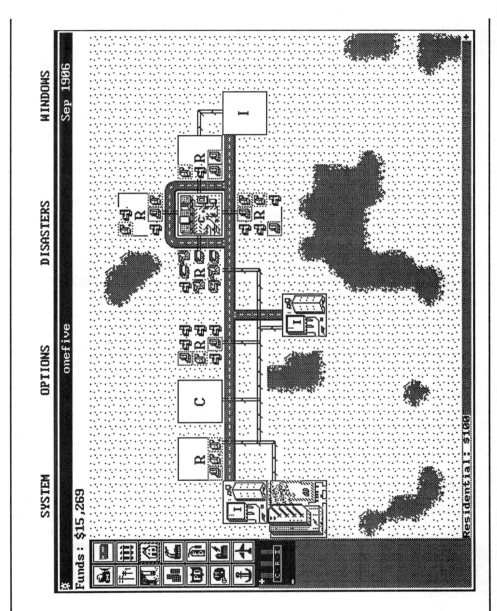

Figure 1-6. Growth factors for commercial zones

Better Living Through Industry: The Industrial Zones Icon

Directly to the right of the Commercial Zones icon is the Industrial Zones icon. Industrial zones represent the manufacturing lifeblood of an urban center. You can designate and develop an industrial zone in exactly the same way you do a residential or commercial zone. The cost to zone an area for industrial development is exactly the same ($100) as it is for a residential or commercial area, and the terrain tiles evolve in similar patterns—in this case, from small tank farms to large warehouses to huge factories.

Industrial zones increase your city's tax base through their own land values and by providing jobs for more residents as they grow. However, industrial zones tend to have lower land values immediately adjacent to them. This is primarily because they stimulate pollution and crime.

In order to test out the negative factors surrounding industrial zones you will need to learn how to activate the evaluation tools described in the "PERT—Program Evaluation and Review Technique" section of this chapter.

Now start a new city and create two industrial zones. Place one industrial zone surrounded by roads and four residential neighborhoods. Place the other industrial zone out by itself, but have a road from four other residential neighborhoods feeding into it. Your screen should look something like Figure 1-7. Let the simulation run for a few years. Now access the Pollution Index map. Notice the lack of pollution near the suburban neighborhoods compared to the pollution found immediately adjacent to the industrial zones themselves. The lesson may be obvious, but it shows that SimCity's model really works.

 Chips on the Old Block: The Police Departments Icon

The Police Departments icon is extremely important in your fight against the ever-rising crime rate. Since adding a police department is going to increase your city's budget considerably, you will want to wait until the crime rate or civic demand forces you to establish such a force. It costs $500 to build a police station and $100 per annum to fund it properly. Full funding will severely reduce crime in the areas near the police station; reduced funding geometrically reduces effectiveness. To build a police station, move the arrow cursor to the icon and click on

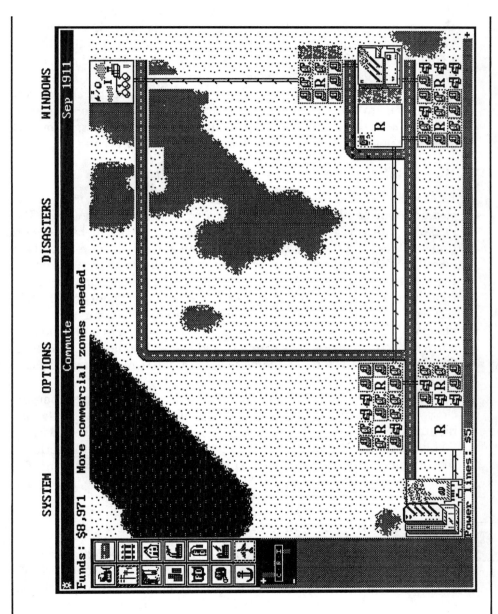

Figure 1-7.　Negative factors surrounding industrial zones

the mouse button or press SPACEBAR.Then scroll the cursor box across the map until you reach the site upon which you wish to locate the police department. Click on the mouse button or press the SPACEBAR to place the building, and follow up by providing power and road or rail access to activate the department.

To create your own inner city crime wave, load the Detroit scenario. Call up the Crime Rate map and notice the current levels of crime. Then gradually reduce the funding for police protection for each year and notice the more than commensurate rise in crime.

 ### Burn, Baby, Burn!: the Fire Departments Icon

Fires will break out in your city just as they do in real cities, and you will certainly not be able to put them out very efficiently without the Fire Departments icon. Even without a fire department, you can bulldoze fire breaks all around the fire and allow it to burn itself out (and burn down everything that happens to be within the fire breaks!). If you do have a fire department, however, there will be a substantially improved fire containment radius (that is, a better chance of putting out the fire). So, since most of the disasters than can befall a city will bring about fires along with their own destructive forces, it's a good idea to build and fund a fire department as soon as your city budget can handle it. The costs for fire departments are the same as for police departments, and the construction procedure is also handled the same way.

If you wish to test the game's accuracy in handling fire emergencies, you can simply build a small city with a fully funded fire department. Save the game. Then, go to the Disasters menu (discussed in the "When It Rains, It Pours Department: The Disasters Menu" section of this chapter) and select Fires. Time how long it takes for the fire department to get the fire out. Then reload the same game, reduce the funding by 50 percent and repeat the procedure.

 ### Fourth and Inches: The Stadiums Icon

Although the Stadiums icon does not exist in the C-64/128 version, it is a useful tool in the other versions. Once your city reaches a fairly large size, you will either receive the equivalent of a scathing newspaper editorial on the message bar ("Residents demand a new stadium") or decide to build a stadium to encourage residential growth and enhance your tax base. Perhaps the best thing about the way SimCity handles the stadium is that you don't have to build luxury boxes in order to keep your "SimFL" team or raise the hotel tax in advance to lure a franchise to your town. You build a stadium in the same way that you construct a police or fire department, but it costs $3,000 to build one. Maintenance costs are presumably covered by ticket revenues, since you do not have to deal with them in your budget. All you have to do is make certain that you have sufficient residential zones to support the stadium, that adequate power supplies the stadium, and that there will be an efficient road and/or transit network to provide access. Once you've accomplished these prerequisites, you'll see an intriguing animation sequence in which the stadium fills and the teams march up and down the field.

 ## Power Pack: The Power Plants Icon

Before your town can ever become operative, you must have some way to provide power. The Power Plants icon offers a simple choice of building either a nuclear power plant or a traditional coal-fired power plant. To build a power plant, simply move the arrow cursor to the Power Plants icon and click. Then you must choose between the coal-burning or nuclear power plant. Some players have complained that SimCity is too generous in allowing nuclear power plants to last until they are around 150 years old. Actually, given that there are nearly 500 reactors that have been operating 20 to 30 years around the world, and figuring a pessimistic five major releases of radiation (which assumes that some were not publicized), one can estimate a figure closer to one incident every 3,000 operating years or so. This means that nuclear reactors melt down more often in SimCity than in real life. They have the advantage of being able to supply three times the amount of electrical power that the coal-powered plant can provide, but they cost $2,000 more to construct ($5,000) and have considerably more dangerous potential consequences.

Of course, there is a trade-off in opting for the less expensive coal-powered plant ($3,000). These are less dangerous, but only support a third of the number of zones that the nuclear plant can support. Further, they are a primary cause of pollution. Many players prefer to start out immediately with nuclear power plants for just these reasons. Note, however, that you begin building your city at the turn of the century. The historical purist will avoid such an easy out, preferring to wait until at least the 1950s to construct a nuclear-powered plant.

You can test out the model by building a coal-powered plant and a nuclear-powered plant at opposite ends of the map. Build a variety of zones in the areas surrounding them and wait a few game years. Then, using the Pollution Index map described in the "PERT—Program Evaluation and Review Technique" section of this chapter, note which area is most affected by pollution. Of course, a nuclear plant offers a considerable amount of deadly pollution if it should melt down, but you are unlikely to discover this in a short scenario like the one just suggested.

 ### Down to the Sea in Ships: The Sea Ports Icon

The Sea Ports icon is used to build a working harbor area so that industrial growth will be spurred upward. Adding a seaport will have little effect on a small city, but once a city has plenty of industrial zones, this addition should accelerate industrial development. It costs $5,000 to zone land for a seaport. You simply move the arrow cursor until it rests on the Sea Ports icon and move the cursor box until it rests over a logical site for a new seaport. It should, of course, be adjacent to a shoreline, but the program's algorithm doesn't really know whether the port is located adjacent to water or not. It simply knows whether the port exists or not.

Once the seaport has power and road or transit access, it will begin to impact industrial growth positively (and add a ship's air horn sound effect, as well as ship animation to the game's audio-visual mix). The downside is that you will have to contend with occasional shipwrecks. Therefore, it is recommended that you do not build a port until you have a definite need for one (except, possibly, to study the historical lesson to be learned in the section "By the Sea: The Role of Ports in American Urban History" in Chapter 2).

 ### The Wild Blue Yonder: The Airports Icon

Where the Sea Ports icon accelerates your city's industrial growth potential, the Airports icon greatly expands your city's commercial growth potential. If you should find that you have a large city where the commercial zones are no longer developing, you may need an airport. You build an airport by moving the arrow cursor to the Airports icon. Then you move the box (cursor) to the location where you wish to construct the airport and click the mouse button or press SPACEBAR. Usually, you will receive a prompt over the message bar stating that the residents want an airport, but regardless, you will want to wait until you have a specific need before you build the airport.

There are several reasons to wait before building your airport. First of all, airports are expensive to zone ($10,000). Second, they create the potential for air disasters. Third, they automatically toggle an annoying traffic helicopter, complete with repetitive traffic reports, onto the scene. (It's cute at first, but it gets old quickly.)

One tip about constructing airports is that you should place the airport so that planes will take off over water whenever possible. This will reduce the probability of air crashes, but experience proves that this is not a foolproof plan. Some planes will inevitably begin to fly over your city and some of these are destined to crash, usually at the most inopportune time.

Load one of the scenario cities and bulldoze enough of it to place an airport near the city's center. Play with the city for a few game years and note how long it takes before there is an air disaster. Then load the same city and place an airport far away from everything (preferably next to the water). Play with the city for a few game years and note how long it takes before there is an air disaster.

Goals to Go!: The Purpose of Urban Planning

By now, some of you are wondering why anyone bothers with urban planning. The game's controls seem relatively simple to use and the decisions to be made seem rather straightforward. Where is the challenge to this game, anyway? This section will attempt to describe some of the problem-solving approaches used by actual urban planners and show how they can apply to your playing experience with SimCity. You should learn something about problem solving, system analysis, and program evaluation in the course of this section.

Urban planning is, essentially, a systematic attempt to provide a higher quality of life for the entire population of a city. Because urban planning is primarily and attempt to solve the *existing* problems in an urban environment, as well as those problems that are likely to arise as a result of growth and expansion, it seems logical to begin by considering where human needs are *not* being met. One quick and dirty method is to utilize an elaborated *needs gap equation*. For example, the existing problem might be traffic congestion. In this case, the planner might realize that lighter traffic is to be desired and observe that there are too many cars for too few roads. The equation might look something like this:

Gap = (Cars per capita x Actual Population) - Road Capacity

Imagine, therefore, a small community in which each family of four has two cars. Imagine also that the community has ten miles of roads that can handle 25 cars per mile (during the rush hour) without severe congestion (that is, a 250-car capacity). If the community grows to a population of 750, the equation looks like this:

(.5 x 750) - 250 = 125

This means that 125 extra cars are clogging the roads.

In the example, the simplistic way to deal with the problem would be to add an additional five miles of road, so that an equilibrium would be reached.

(.5 x 750) - 375 = 0

Of course, this very simple equation does not consider that fact that not all of the 375 cars would necessarily be on the ten-mile road network at the same time. It certainly does not take into consideration that building new roads might encourage further population growth, which would in turn reopen the needs gap. It does not take into account the option of financing a village bus to handle the rush hour or of encouraging a concerted effort to carpool. Some government agencies seem to opt for such simple equations, failing to adequately take the interdependence of certain factors into account.

A more sophisticated view of urban planning realizes that the aesthetic appeal of a city, the logical arrangement of transportation networks combined with need-oriented zones, the provision for public safety and sanitation, and the establishment of community services are all an organic part of urban development. In SimCity, your effectiveness at all of these tasks is measured by a dynamic score (with a maximum of 1,000 points) based on four groups of factors. These include

- *Human factors* These include adequate housing and amenities, job availability, and environmental quality.

- *Economic factors*   These include land value, number of industrial and commercial zones, unemployment rate, internal and external markets, amount of taxation, and appropriate funding for community services.
- *Survival factors*   These include crime rate, pollution index and disaster management.
- *Political factors*   These include public opinion on the city's problems ("Sim"plistic evaluations, no doubt) and the mayor's popularity and responsiveness to civic demands.

PERT—Program Evaluation and Review Technique

It is possible to monitor these concerns through a series of tools provided within the program. On most systems, the simplest method of gauging your progress as mayor of SimCity is to call up the Evaluation window. On the Amiga, IBM, and Macintosh, you can access the Evaluation window by pulling down the Windows menu with the mouse and clicking on either Evaluation (Macintosh) or Eval (Amiga). If you have an IBM with no mouse, you can either press W while holding down the ALT key (ALT-W) to access the Evaluation window from the Windows menu shown here (IBM versions),

WINDOWS

Maps	Ctrl-M
Graphs	Ctrl-G
Budget	Ctrl-B
Edit	Ctrl-E
Evaluation	Ctrl-U
Close	Ctrl-C
Hide	Ctrl-H
Position	Ctrl-P
Resize (Edit)	Ctrl-R

or press U while holding down the CTRL key to call up the Evaluation window immediately. (IBM and Tandy users can also simply press F5 to open the Windows menu.) The C-64/128 version offers a number of graphs, but no such succinct evaluation of your progress (or regress).

The Evaluation window (shown in Figure 1-8) provides you with a simple opinion poll that gives the mayor's approval rating in percentages and presents the city's worst problems in order of importance. This

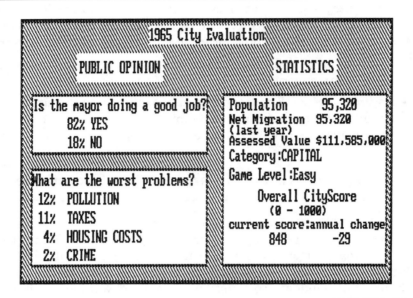

Figure 1-8. The Evaluation window

window shows the current population and net migration to or from your city, assessed value of the aggregate property in the community, and the overall city score (ranging from 0 to 1,000).

You will find the public opinion polls given in the Evaluation window to be of the utmost value in prioritizing your activities as mayor. For example, if housing or housing costs are your citizen's primary concerns, you shouldn't be zoning commercial and industrial areas at that point in time. If housing in general is the primary concern, for example, you should be approving more residential zones. If housing costs are the problem, however, you will need to approve more residential zones in areas where property values are lower.

In order to implement the last suggestion, you will need to use some other tools, available through the Maps window. The Maps window shown in Figure 1-9 can be accessed on most machines by means of the Windows menu, in the same way that you accessed the Evaluation window. In order to reach these maps on the C-64/128 version, you will need to highlight the Map Screen icon and press the

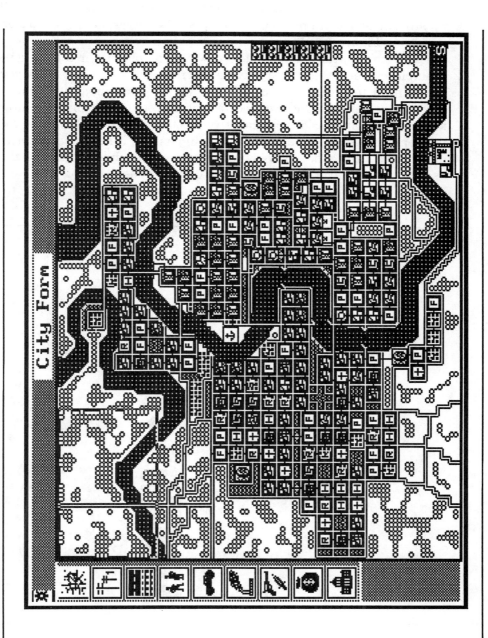

Figure 1-9. The Maps window

joystick button. Once you have reached the Maps window, you can call up any one of several maps by clicking on the corresponding map icon (shown in Figure 1-10).

The maps can assist you in several ways. For instance, in the previous example, in which the primary problem in the city was housing costs, you would need to access the Land Value map to find areas with lower assessed valuations. Once you located these areas, it is a simple matter to establish some residential zones to meet this need. If, however, the problem were simply a lack of housing in general, it might be better to locate residential zones in areas with higher land values to increase the assessed valuation of the city and add to the tax base.

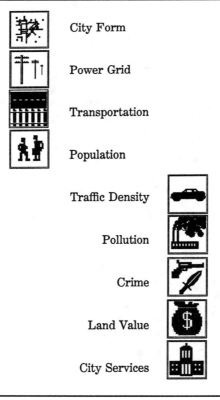

City Form

Power Grid

Transportation

Population

Traffic Density

Pollution

Crime

Land Value

City Services

Figure 1-10. The Maps window icons

Another screen that can be of assistance in your planning is the City Form map. This map screen will assist you in observing the shape of your evolving city, and it can guide you in planning further expansion by allowing you to see available terrain at a glance. You may want to make certain that your highest polluting zones are located on the edge of the map. In this way, only half of the pollution is measured against your city; the rest is blown (figuratively speaking) off the edge of the map and into the neighboring community. Although this may not seem realistic at the outset, it is valid in the same way that some metropolitan cities have to contend not only with their own pollution, but with second-hand smog from larger cities upwind of their city.

Macintosh users have some additional choices on the City Forms map. On the Mac, the program offers a submenu with four choices. The player can opt to see all zones, commercial zones only, residential zones only, or industrial zones only. On the Amiga, there is a separate map icon that you can select in order to display the three types of zones in distinct colors.

Assume, then, that your city is experiencing blackouts and power breaks. The greatest way to locate them is to access the Power Grid map. If, on the other hand, the crime rate is the biggest problem, you can focus on the problem by accessing the Crime Rate map. The same is true of the Traffic Density map.

The Population Maps icon offers two different map screens that can be toggled in the same way you toggled between coal and nuclear power on the Power Plants icon. (Amiga users have separate icons for the two maps.) The Population Density map shows how many people actually occupy or utilize a given area of the city, while the Rate of Growth map shows how fast a given area is growing. On these maps you can observe where the growth needs to be slowed or where to avoid further development.

The same style of toggle is used on the City Services map. You can toggle between the Fire Protection map, which will help you know where to locate future fire stations in order to provide the most effective radius of fire protection, and the Police Influence map, which will help you reduce crime by locating police precincts at proper confluences of need. (Again, Amiga users have separate icons for the Fire Protection and Police Influence maps.)

You can also call up the Pollution Index map. This will help you identify the areas of your city where pollution needs to be reduced (or, at least, not augmented). Another map that may be of value is the Transportation map, which helps you determine what portions of your city need better access by road or rail to other areas of the city.

Once you have learned to use all of these informative maps, you may want to access the game's graphs. On the Amiga, IBM, and Macintosh these can be called up through the Windows menu in the same way as the other tools. On the IBM, you can access them by pressing CTRL-G. With the C-64/128 version, you simply highlight the Graph Screen icon and press the joystick button. All versions have graphs that show changes in population, commercial, and industrial size, and fluctuations in the crime rate and cash flow of the community (see Figure 1-11). Except for the C-64/128, all versions have a pollution graph available as well.

Finally, you will need to become familiar with the Fiscal Budget window, the game's version of that favorite tool of all bureaucrats, the budget. The Fiscal Budget window appears automatically at the end of every fiscal year in game time, but it can also be accessed at any time on the IBM by pressing CRTL-B or through the Windows menu. When this window appears (see Figure 1-12), you have the power to raise, maintain, or (heaven forfend!) lower taxes. In addition, you have the power to line item veto up to the full funding of any of three city departments.

Urban planners usually employ three basic sets of criteria when evaluating the effectiveness of a program or policy. First, they attempt to identify all the impacts of a program or policy over a fair period of time. Second, they judge the impacts with regard to their having a positive or negative effect on the environment, community, or population. Third, they evaluate the cost-effectiveness of the program or policy in light of the first two sets of criteria.

These criteria should be useful as you try to determine whether or not you are manipulating the right resources to meet your city's needs. If, for example, your nuclear power plant keeps melting down before you get your city to the size you want, it is *not* the solution to the problems involved in the trade-off between pollution and the need for electrical power. Several coal-fired plants on the outskirts of the map

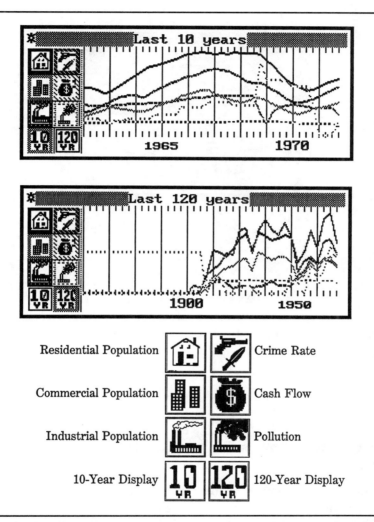

Figure 1-11. A 10- and 120-year evaluation graph with all graphs on

may offer a more permanent and less dangerous solution which may be more cost-effective in the long run.

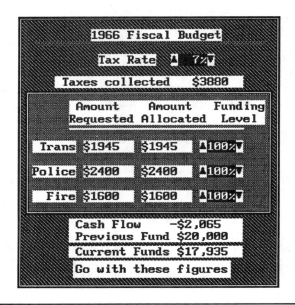

Figure 1-12. The Fiscal Budget window

When It Rains, It Pours Department: The Disasters Menu

If you feel like you're ready for an expert-level challenge in crisis management, SimCity has a built-in mechanism for delivering this exhilarating experience. This mechanism is called the Disasters menu. The C-64/128 version offers a menu of four disasters (Fire, Tornado, Monster, and/or Earthquake), which can be selected in order to wreak havoc upon your city. On the C-64/128, simply highlight the Disaster menu icon from the Edit Window screen and press the joystick button. If you are using one of the other machines, simply pull down the Disasters menu shown in the following.

```
┌─────────────────────┐
│ DISASTERS           │
│ ┌─────────────────┐ │
│ │ Fire            │ │
│ │ Flood           │ │
│ │ Air Crash       │ │
│ │ Tornado         │ │
│ │ Earthquake      │ │
│ │ Monster         │ │
│ │ ─────────       │ │
│ │▶Disable         │ │
│ └─────────────────┘ │
└─────────────────────┘
```

and select from an enlarged roster of disasters. In addition to those available on the C-64/128, the other versions feature air crashes, earthquakes, floods, shipwrecks, and tornadoes. Although these disasters will occur randomly throughout your city's history, there may be times when you wish to test your disaster preparedness or simply bring about unwarranted destruction for one reason or another.

In one office, four colleagues were competing against each other to see who could build the best city from scratch. Once day, the worker with the least seniority brought in the most magnificent city map any of them had yet developed. Although the coworkers admired the craftsmanship of their colleague's city, a wicked idea flashed through their minds when the would-be city architect left the room for about ten minutes. "Why don't we toggle on all the possible disasters simultaneously?" They saved the city to another disk so that they wouldn't actually lose the coworker's labor. Then they inserted the original data disk and actually performed this atrocity, watching idly and contentedly as air crashes, monster attacks, fires, and earthquakes reduced almost seven-eighths of the beautiful city to rubble. Then they saved the rubble on their colleague's original disk so that he would think his marvelous city was lost. Fortunately, they gave him the back-up save disk before any of them looked like the battered map of his city.

What Do the "Sim"ple Folk Do?

This chapter was intended to give you a basic understanding of the SimCity editing tools, as well as provide some useful notes on the way they are used in the SimCity model. It should also have introduced you to some simple principles used by urban planners and suggested some ways to emulate these approaches in SimCity. Armed with this information, you should be able to build more efficient and realistic cities which will enable you both to achieve a higher score and to derive satisfaction from playing the game.

If you are interested in a brief history of urban planning, or wish to examine thoroughly some of the problems faced by contemporary urban planners, you may want to read further and explore the simple scenarios, exercises, and problems provided in the remainder of this book. Hopefully, SimCity will continue to be "sim"ply fascinating as you discover more and more why the "Sims" (and sometimes you'll want to call them "Sim"pletons) do what they do!

CHAPTER 2
I LOVE A HISTORY: URBAN PLANNING IN THE PAST

City planning is largely a result of the human desire for order. Even the earliest ages of communal living showed some degree of order and city design. Whether this order evolved informally or was formally decreed by a hierarchy (priestly, military, or monarchical), it seems to have followed a general purpose. This chapter will delineate some of those purposes.

This chapter presents a brief sketch of the historical development of cities. It will move swiftly from the basic concepts at work in the evolution of older cities to those concepts that particularly influenced the development of cities in North America. Because SimCity is based mainly on forces seen in the latter cities, the second section is expected to be of more value to the SimCity player. Nevertheless, it helps to know something about the development of cities in general if you expect to make intelligent decisions about the development of your city in particular.

Classical Grasp: Early Cities

In the ancient Near East, defensive considerations played a primary role in the evolution of cities. In general, cities were built on top of hills (called *tells*), and they were fortified with walls. The invention of the battering ram toward the end of the Early Bronze Age forced a Middle Bronze Age redesign, adding a *fosse* (or pit) and an intermediary *rampart* at the bottom of the tell, while the main walls were higher up. The point of central importance for the Near Eastern city was usually placed on the highest prominence. This locale could be a temple, fortress, palace, or a combination of the three. The rest of the city grew in relation to this citadel.

In Book VII of his *Politics*, Aristotle suggests that the design of a city should reflect its government. For example, an oligarchy or monarchy needs an acropolis for its fortress temple or citadel. An aristocracy, on the other hand, would require a large number of less accessible, easily defended places. Finally, a democracy would need a plain where many residences could be built on the same level. He goes on to note that cities designed as regular grid patterns are more convenient for those who live there, but he contends that cities need some clumps of irregular streets in order to confuse and entrap invaders in times of war. In this he goes against the grain of Hippodamus, the fifth century B.C. designer of Miletus, who is often called the father of the gridiron plan (see Figure 2-1).

By the time of the Roman Empire's greatest expansion, another model built on defensive considerations had taken hold (see Figure 2-2). To a large degree, this city plan was influenced by the severe grid structure used in the Roman army camp of the middle to late Roman Republic era (from the middle of the third century to the late first century B.C.).

When the Roman Republic was expanding, the Roman army marched from daybreak to midday. They would spend the remainder of the afternoon constructing a fortified camp, and they would spend the entire evening recuperating from the exertion. This gave the Roman army the advantageous capability of retreating to a fortified encampment and returning to bring battle with rested troops on the very next day.

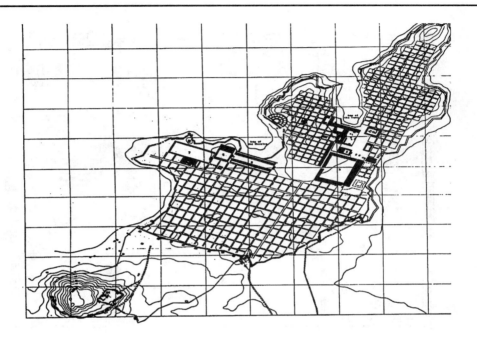

Figure 2-1. Ground plan of Miletus (Asia Minor, fifth century B.C.)

Because most of the early administrators of conquered territories were men of military experience, it is no wonder that many towns and cities were built or rebuilt following the pattern of the Roman military camps.

Classics Illustrated: Applying the Lessons

To a large extent, these early patterns demonstrate the two basic forms of urban development. Cities either radiate outward from a control point (in concentric circles, semicircles, radial spokes, or a combination of these) or form a grid-like geometrical pattern. These layouts are determined, primarily, by the need for access to various locations, so they are often referred to as *transportation alternatives.*

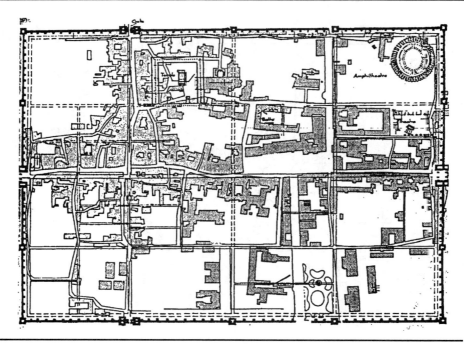

Figure 2-2. Ground plan of Aosta (Italy, first century B.C.)

An extreme use of the geometrical grid can be seen in the basic street plan of London prior to the Great Fire of 1666 (Figure 2-3). This is largely attributable to Roman influence. London was founded during the Claudian invasion of 43 A.D. (as Londinium), when the Romans built both a bridge and a fortified city. Upstream, the City of Westminster was founded as another Roman settlement. Over the centuries, the two cities grew together (Westminster as a royal and religious center, and London as a commercial center) with nobles and priests residing between the two towns. Because both towns began as rectilinear cities, they evolved as an extension of their Roman origin. In fact, Cheapside and Cannon Streets were simply medieval extensions to the east-west roads used by the Romans.

While playing SimCity, you can duplicate, to some extent, the way Londinium and Westminster grew together. You simply build two power

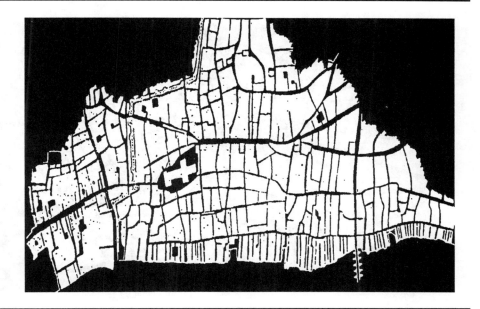

Figure 2-3. London before the Great Fire (1666)

plants and two population centers on the same side of the main body of water on your map. Let both mini-cities grow for a couple of years; then build a long stretch of road between the two centers (this represents The Strand, Fleet Street, and Cannon Street). Then, as your city develops, note how efficient it is to place plenty of residential zones adjacent to the long road. This is a simplified version of how London developed.

Radial designs, on the other hand, emphasize thoroughfares or avenues (in a traditional plan) or transit routes (in a more modern plan). The original city of Karlsruhe, West Germany, is an example of radial design (see Figure 2-4). Karlsruhe was built circa 1715 with most of the city located in concentric circles radiating outward from the medieval castle. The city was designed in this way to visually suggest circles of influence emanating from the prince.

SimCity does not allow road and rail lines to be placed diagonally, so you will not be able to implement exactly urban designs that use diagonals as thoroughfares to bring the main traffic flow to the center of a

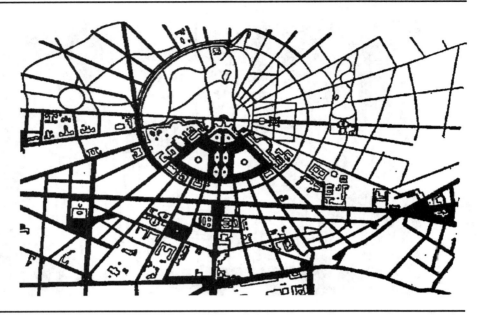

Figure 2-4. Ground plan of Karlsruhe, Germany

city. However, you can use a series of right angles to approximate a radial city. Cities that you design in SimCity in which neighborhoods are built at a distance from the industrial center and traffic is brought into the city center via roads or rail will not be as geometrically pure as L'Enfant's diagonals in Washington, D.C. (see Figure 2-5). However, the difficulties you will go through in using a series of right angles to emulate this style will underscore the most severe problem with this approach to urban design. That is, essentially, that diagonal thorough-fares to the important points in a city tend to cut portions of the city into irregular shapes that are often less useful than the rectangles on a grid. In a nation's capital, where there is an emphasis on the ceremonial and monumental, that may not be a problem. These irregular plots can be put to use for aesthetic purposes. In most cities, however, there is no real need or desire for this proliferation of irregular shapes.

One very useful possibility for the radial city concept, within the parameters of SimCity, is to put the first power plant and the bulk of

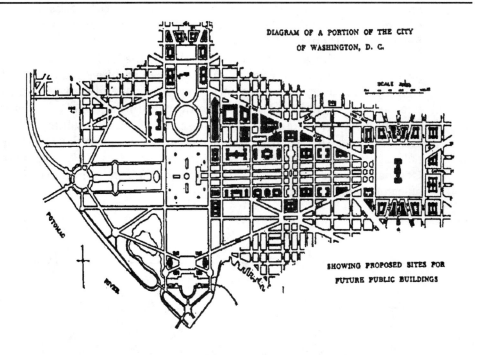

Figure 2-5. L'Enfant's plan for Washington, D.C.

the industrial zones at the center of your terrain. Then place your residential zones at the edges of the map. Funnel the traffic into the city center using a series of right angles until the city center is starting to grow. Then, as a buffer between the heavy industrial pollutants and the virtually smog-free suburban countryside, you can plant a *greenbelt* (although considering the square shapes of the terrain tiles, perhaps "green boundary" is more correct). After creating the greenbelt, you should still have plenty of space to construct a commercial belt. In this way, you will have implemented some of the radial city design. You will find that it makes for a fairly efficient city in the long run. In the short run, you will find that it is more expensive than the strict, geometrical grid pattern.

The grid pattern is the easiest transportation option to implement. However, you will notice that it is less distinctive than the radial city and offers less opportunity to exploit or to sculpt the particular terrain of a cityscape. Notice the extreme regularity of colonial Williamsburg, for example (Figure 2-6).

Let's note, however, what Le Corbusier, the Swiss architect who so profoundly affected the French and American architects of the twentieth century, had to say about geometric regularity: "Man walks in a straight line because he has a goal and knows where he's going .... The pack donkey meanders along ... takes the path of least resistance .... Man must consider the result in advance .... But the pack donkey thinks of nothing at all, except what will save himself trouble." This said, Le Corbusier suggests that pure, straight geometrical forms are the most efficient shapes for human living.

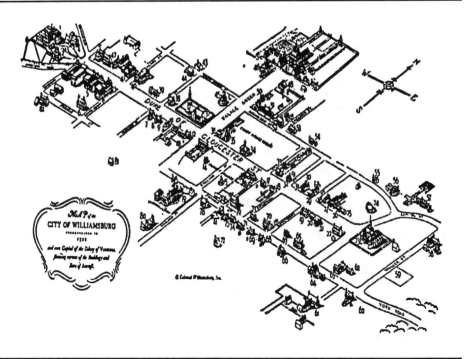

Figure 2-6.   Sketch of colonial Williamsburg

By the Sea: The Role of Ports in American Urban History

Beyond geometric considerations, urban planners are also constrained to consider the uses of the land itself. In general, land use alternatives are determined by the available terrain. The first type of development with regard to land use is that of *continuous expansion*. In this type of development, the urban center begins at a certain point and grows outward to meet increasing needs, and it usually ends up expanding wherever physically possible.

In American urban history, the port was the physical point from which the urban center began to expand. At the time of the Revolutionary War, the cities of Boston, New York, and Philadelphia were virtually synonymous with their harbors. The port was the commercial, communications, and industrial center of the early American cities. The port was valuable largely as a point of access to the Old World. Imports of manufactured goods were brought to American shores by ships, which, in exchange, sent American resources to European ports. Neighborhoods full of warehouses grew up around the ports to store the imported goods and raw materials. In turn, commercial buildings for wholesale brokerage and retail appeared nearby. Wealthy neighborhoods grew up in the vicinity, because owners needed to be fairly close to their holdings. Lower-cost housing proliferated because of the need for dockworkers, warehousemen, and other laborers.

As the functions surrounding this initial center of development grew, there was considerable pressure for additional and affordable housing. Fortunately, there was sufficient transportation during the nineteenth century (when the emerging railroads combined with horsecar lines and ferry operations) that many families began to discover less expensive housing sites beyond the boundaries of the original city. Not only was the American suburb discovered as a solution to the need for affordable housing, but the absence of urban crowding and the improvement over urban sanitation gave those pioneers who moved to the suburbs a feeling that they had attained a higher quality of life.

Although it is not the optimal plan for developing your own city, you can simulate an early American city's history in SimCity. In this scenario, you establish your initial zones at the shoreline and construct a seaport earlier than is normally required. The SimCity model doesn't really let you take advantage of the seaport until your city has reached a certain size, so you will be less efficient during the early stages of the game than you would normally be. However, you should discover some of the problems that faced early American cities by attempting this approach.

Begin by placing your coal-fired power plant near the shoreline. Then build the seaport, an industrial zone, and a couple of residential zones and connect them all via roads and power lines. Beginning with this nucleus, you will notice that you tend to expand outward in a semicircle from the harbor area. You will also notice that, rather than the orderly pattern you normally strive for when playing SimCity, you often end up with a patchwork of commercial, industrial, and residential zones that are plopped down rather quickly as you try to meet particular needs, crises, and demands. Interestingly enough, this is precisely what was happening in the United States around 1870.

In "The American City: What shaped its development?", Thomas Bender describes this phenomenon: "Beyond this center-city cluster of commercial and residential space, the bulk of the city [New York, 1870] extended perhaps three or four miles into a kind of ragged and mixed-use cityscape marked by pockets of commercial, industrial, and residential uses. While one could call this fringe area confused, it is more precise to call it ill-defined and literally undistinguished urban space." Bender goes on to indicate how the development of the urban sky-scraper eased some of the urban sprawl problem at this point. Fortunately, the SimCity model does have the capacity to rebuild commercial and residential zones to take advantage of vertical space.

In *The Economy of Cities*, American economist Jane Jacobs tells about the history of Detroit as a manufacturing power. She observes that flour was the city's primary export in the 1820s and 1830s and that a complete economy of grist mills, docks, taverns, and workshops grew up to support that export-based economy. In time, machine shops grew up around the mills to repair the mill machinery. Then, because the ships that transported the flour needed to be built and repaired, ship-yards grew up around the flour- and machinery-based economy. Later, because of acquired skills and the availability of labor, these same shipyards began to build ocean-worthy steamships.

By the 1860s, Detroit was no longer primarily a flour-milling city—it was an exporter of marine engines. Between 1860 and 1880, the economy shifted to refining copper from local sources of ore. Originally, this copper refining was designed to support the local machine shops by providing the raw materials for brass valves and fittings. Then the city began to export the refined copper as well. By the time the ore was no longer available in quantities necessary for export (1880), Detroit had diversified into a full-scale manufacturing town. It is no wonder that it became the home of the automobile industry. The economy was there to support a major new manufacturing effort like automobile production.

In the present era, however, Detroit has had a rather stagnant economy, primarily because of its dependence on the automobile industry. You can avoid this phenomenon in SimCity by being certain to add an airport or seaport, along with enough commercial zones, before the city becomes totally dependent on its industrial capacity. In SimCity, as in actuality, a city without an export capacity is in fatal trouble.

The Tell-Tale Plot: Grid Patterns in American Urban Development

The easiest plan to emulate in SimCity is the gridiron (sometimes called the chessboard) plan. It greatly affected American urban development in that surveyors and planners from seventeenth century Williamsburg and Philadelphia through the midwestern towns of the nineteenth century utilized this method. According to the gridiron plan, the city area was surveyed and divided into a number of rectangular plots. One major advantage of this practice was that the regular size of the plots permitted prospective buyers to consider purchasing the property, even if they had never visited the actual location of the town.

The practice of designing *speculator's towns* continued to the point where developers all along the railroads utilized a *standard town plat* (see Figure 2-7). These plans enabled developers like Illinois Associates (planners of towns along the route of the Illinois Central Railroad) to simply write in the name of a new town at the top of the generic map and the plan was completed. This had the advantage of being quick, but it had the disadvantage of creating towns that completely ignored terrain features. In addition, the purchasers of various plots had a tendency to ignore the need for open spaces and often ended up building from lot line to lot line.

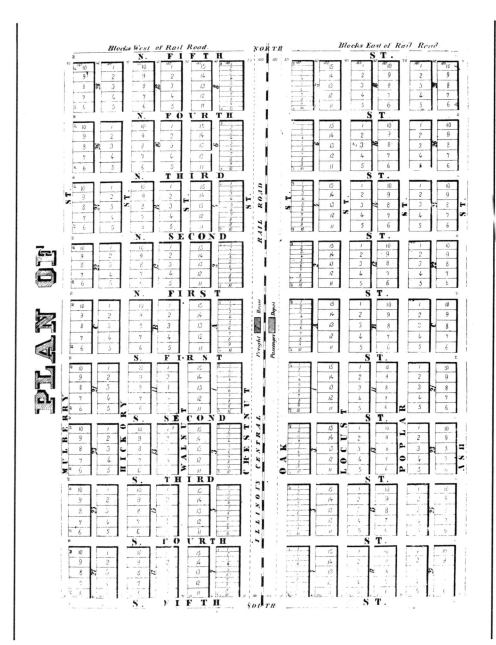

Figure 2-7. Standard town plat (with permission, Baker Library, Harvard Business School)

Zoned In: Efficiency in Urban Planning

In the United States, New York City was the very first urban area to divide an entire community into zones or districts determined by the present or potential use of a given property. An ordinance to this effect was passed in 1916. A New York City engineer of that era, Frank Koester, stated the rationale behind zoning in his *Modern City Planning and Maintenance*, " ... the objects to be accomplished are the providing of healthful living and working conditions, prevention of congestion, convenience of distribution, suitable relation of the homes of the workers to their places of employment, and the grouping together of those whose incomes and tastes are generally similar."

These areas of functionality still hold largely true, although the latter phrase seems to harbor a latent racism. By 1930, several hundred local governments had followed suit and established similar ordinances. Zoning accomplishes the conservation of property value, the provision of a plan for ordered growth, and the protection of public welfare.

The Green, Green Grass of Home: Open Spaces in Urban Planning

Another land use alternative is *nucleated expansion*. Under this model, city clusters grow up around various geographic features. For example, early on in the industrialization of the U.S., *industrial satellite* cities began to form around waterfalls (which provided power to drive machinery). Later, the invention of the steam engine allowed these industrial clusters to move closer to the city center.

The modern urban planner will often utilize the nucleated expansion principle to take advantage of particular terrain features. For example, in planning the community of Greendale, Wisconsin during the mid-1930s, an architectural team observed that the scenic west side of the community was an ideal place to reserve for housing that would attract high-income residents. Therefore, they designed that side of the city using a scheme that allowed maximum space per lot and used the natural terrain to advantage. This philosophy can be implemented in SimCity in order to build an upper-class residential zone, which will keep the tax base high. Simply look for islands that are large enough to be zoned as residential or wooded areas that can border residential zones on one or more sides. Place the zones and connect them for road access and power. Then, to be certain they don't "go condo," bulldoze one corner and plant a park to ensure that the zone does not overbuild. You certainly cannot afford to perform this cosmetic surgery on every residential zone, but it will ensure a fashionable Beverly Hills-style area for your city with proportionately high land values.

Another principle utilized in Greendale, according to Elbert Peets (former lecturer on urban planning at both Harvard and Yale, as well as one of the architects of the Greendale plan), was that a low gross density justifies a relatively high average net density in terms of population. In order to achieve this, the team designed functional open spaces. Service roads were designed with greenery on each side so that they did not *appear* to be alleys. Pedestrian walkways were separated from the streets. Finally, houses were set opposite each other so that they were closer together on more affordable lots, but were provided with both a shared openness and a small backyard for purposes of privacy.

You cannot place the individual houses in SimCity, but you can achieve the effect of net population growth with a reasonable population density by being creative with open spaces. Do not hesitate to plant parks around roads and transit lines, and in any small, irregular plots. This will have the positive effect of increasing land value and indirectly affecting the quality of life through reducing crime.

Sometimes, using the terrain in this way indicates that the city will grow amoeba-like, with tendrils extending in various directions to make use of certain terrain, while avoiding other terrain.

It is not clear that this method can be of use within the SimCity model, except with regard to flood plains. Although flooding is basically a random disaster, you may find it valuable to avoid squares where floods recur. After a flood, it may be wise to convert the affected area, if possible, to parks and avoid repetition of the disaster. This is not always practical, but it can be a useful strategy.

Another area to reserve for open space and parks is immediately adjacent to the airport. In spite of the fact that air crashes are random events, it seems best to avoid putting any development immediately adjacent to the airport (with the possible exceptions of its own power plant and fire department to protect against the loss of the entire airport in the event of a disaster, as described on pages 140-141).

At the present time, American urban development is experiencing the phenomenon of *exurbia*. Telecommuters and individuals with flex hours have moved even farther away from urban centers in order to experience a higher quality of life, and they have transformed many small rural cities and towns into "Yuppievilles." This is a fascinating turn of events, which will be dealt with, to some extent, in Chapter 7 in connection with a rapidly developing area in Southern California. However, it cannot be appropriately emulated using the current SimCity model.

SimCity is extremely well-suited to depict growth struggles, economic tradeoffs due to urban growth, and environmental issues that small cities face in their rapid metamorphosis into urban centers. Although the program cannot simulate all of the fragile decision points in this evolutionary process, it can certainly provide a stimulating overview of the process.

CHAPTER 3

THE POPULATION BOMB: HUMAN RESOURCES AND PROBLEMS

A Chinese proverb reads: "Of all things, people are the most precious." Human resources are a double-edged sword, however. A concentrated population can be an asset, enhancing production and trade, or a liability, contributing to crime, pollution, and excess consumption. It is estimated that the current world population is increasing by over 200,000 people per day. This means that by the year 2000 an additional 2 billion people will have been added to the global population, equivalent to adding urban centers of approximately 5 million in population every 20 days for the rest of the decade. Such unprecedented growth is placing equally unprecedented demands on the world's resources. Alvin Toffler, in *The Third Wave*, has compared the consumption of 87 quadrillion BTUs (British Thermal Units) of energy in the mid-1950s with the incredible figure of 260 quadrillion BTUs in 1980 as one example of the insatiable global demand for resources.

This chapter will consider the double-edged sword of human resources in the context of urban planning and how it can be applied in SimCity. A brief discussion of how urban planners model population growth, along with some observations on how the SimCity model handles population changes, should give you some concrete ideas on what to do about population density, crime, and the quality of life in your own urban simulations.

Up with People: Population Growth Projections

Most urban planners begin with the realization that changes in population result from birth, death, and migration. Perhaps the simplest way to represent population trends is the *residual method.* In this method, the planner takes the last census data for a city, tabulates the actual births and deaths over enough time to establish a birth and mortality rate, projects an estimated population based on birth and mortality, and subtracts that estimate from the actual population. The residual figure becomes the *estimated migration rate.* Although this method tends to underestimate migration, it does show population patterns very quickly.

Another technique, the *vital rates* method, correlates the birth and mortality rates of a larger area (a county, state, or region) with the local population in order to project future growth. Again, it does not estimate migration closely enough to be anything more than a "quick and dirty" calculation.

A very useful technique, known as the *cohort-survival method,* is often used to make population projections in situations where migration is a limited factor. In this approach, the population is divided into categories by sex and age. Individuals belonging to the same statistical category are known as *cohorts.* Age-specific birth and mortality rates are applied, and a pyramid is developed that adds new births at the bottom as other cohorts are aged upward. This enables planners to anticipate age-specific needs as regards housing, health care, schooling, and so on (see Figure 3-1).

In SimCity, you have a much easier job than the typical urban planner. You do not have to worry about the death rate, because the birth rate is always positive. That leaves only the migration problem to consider. Because your score depends on both how large and how

World population 1980 and 2000 projected

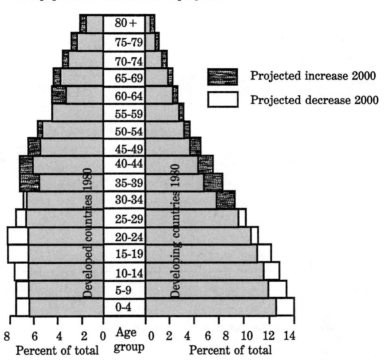

Figure 3-1.   Cohort-survival chart

effective your city is, you will need to be certain that you are not losing population irresponsibly.

For the People: Managing Land Value

The fundamental factor in the way SimCity handles population is called the rent/bid gradient. This principle essentially asserts that the closer a

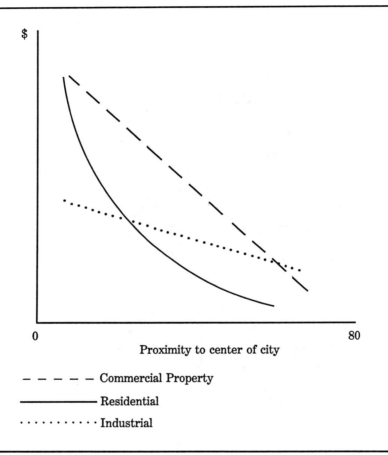

Figure 3-2.   The rent/bid gradient

plot of land is to the center of urban development (represented on the SimCity map), the more valuable it is (see Figure 3-2). In real life, this follows logically from the fact that people who live close to where they work and shop have lower transportation costs, hence more buying power and time.

In SimCity, you can observe this principle by means of a simple experiment.

1. Boot the game and select the Start A New City option.

2. In one corner of the map, build a power plant and zone for an industrial development.

3. Zone for two residential developments. One residential development should be in the extreme corner of the Close-Up Map window, and the other should be very close to the projected industrial development.

4. Build power lines from the power plant to within one space of each of the residential zones, and build roads from the industrial zone to within one space of each of the residential zones.

5. Connect the final road sections to both zones.

6. Connect the power to the residential zone farthest from the industrial zone first, followed by the one nearest the industrial zone.

Notice that the residential zone nearest the industrial zone will grow faster than the zone farther away.

This is not always as simple in reality as it is in SimCity. The SimCity model posits an *isotropic transport plane.* This means that distances are measured on an ideal plane where everything is equally accessible. The program simply checks for distance from the average geographical center of the population to determine land value (which, in turn, determines whether the zone is growing, stagnant, or declining through decay and migration).

In actuality, the accessibility of a given urban center from a residential location is affected by terrain and transportation factors (availability of transport, amount of traffic or passenger density, commute time, and commute cost). People do not create mental maps of their urban areas to scale. Instead, they place landmarks on their maps based on their *perceptions* of distance, which are largely determined by their memory of the difficulty in getting to each landmark. Because there are so many variables involved in this process, SimCity simplifies the problem by using the isotropic transport plane.

In the quick experiment suggested as a test for the rent/bid gradient, there were no commercial zones added to the mix of services for the economy. In terms of game play, however, SimCity requires a balance between the number of industrial, commercial, and residential zones in order to maximize the availability of jobs. Every month, in game time, the program evaluates each residential zone in terms of land value, availability of jobs, and a quality of life quotient that considers pollution, crime, parks, and accessibility. An efficient, high-scoring city will try to keep all of these factors in balance.

People Who Need People: Commercial Considerations

The rent/bid gradient is even steeper for commercial developments than it is for residential properties. In SimCity, as in real life, location is a dominant factor in determining the viability of a commercial development. The program evaluates commercial zones based on a *radius of influence*. Each commercial zone is evaluated according to the accessibility of customers (residential zones), a hidden variable representing an *internal market share* (not in the Commodore version), and the overall balance between commercial, industrial, and residential zones.

The necessity for balance reflects an authentic economic principle known as the *export multiplier effect*. A well-integrated manufacturing center not only produces income from the export of manufactured goods, but its economy is stimulated as new imports return to the manufacturing center. Some of these new imports could be raw materials or machines to enhance production in the exporting industry, but other imports will enlarge the rest of the manufacturing center's economy by becoming part of a local support industry's manufacturing chain (for example, machine parts for a local mechanic to use in repairing the exporting manufacturer's machines or in building new machines) or by entering the wholesale and retail economy. In the case of the former, the local economy will very likely be enlarged when the local supplier decides to export his machinery or expertise to another manufacturing center. Then his exports generate new imports, which add further to the local economy's growth momentum.

There is another multiplier effect, which takes place when a local economy begins to manufacture items to replace those items that the manufacturing center once only imported. This is called the *import replacing multiplier effect*. This principle states simply that when an urban center begins to produce those items that it once imported, it creates a larger economy by virtue of establishing greater demand. For example, a city that imports textiles begins to develop its own textile industry. This creates an influx of textile workers who must, in turn, purchase clothes made from some of the fabrics produced in the local economy. Hence, the internal demand for textiles has exceeded the amount that used to be imported. Other factors, such as reduced transportation costs and increased supply, reduce the basic prices entered into this growth figure, but the point is valid nonetheless.

In SimCity, you only need to manage the export multiplier effect. Here are a few guidelines for your consideration. In actual city economies, a city that is primarily a manufacturing center may use nearly 70 percent of its industrial production for supplying *external* markets, and a city that is primarily a commercial center may use nearly 60 percent of its commercial production to support *internal* markets.

Because it is the support of the internal market that really makes a city take off economically, it should be your goal to reach commercial center status at the earliest possible moment. In SimCity, the external/internal market ratio starts out at 3:1 (the external market is three times greater than the internal market). As the city's size increases, the ratio is reduced to 2:1 and then 1:1 before it finally flip-flops to 1:2, and so forth. In cities in general, the multiplier generally gains momentum at around 200,000 total population. In SimCity, the multiplier usually kicks in earlier and really starts to accelerate when the total population is between 200,000 and 500,000.

A city that produces more for its internal market than it does for the external market is actually more self-sufficient and, consequently, less vulnerable to external market conditions. SimCity simplifies matters by arbitrarily deciding that all commercial production is for the internal market and all industrial production for the external market.

SimCity's documentation states that the ideal balance between zones is for the sum of commercial and industrial zones to equal the total number of residential zones. The preceding discussion indicates that you should have more industrial zones than commercial zones during the early history of your city and more commercial zones than industrial zones when you reach the metropolis stage.

Industrial Strength Planner: Industrial Considerations

The SimCity program evaluates industrial zones with far less complex calculations than those related to commercial and residential zones.

When the industrial zone is evaluated, the program simply wants to know whether the zone is connected to the power grid or not and whether your "Sims" can get to work or not. The zone is upgraded or downgraded on that basis and the result of that function is looped back into the calculation for evaluating residential zones (which, in turn, causes a ripple effect through the entire model). You should also remember that there is a point in the game when you will need a seaport in order to support full industrial development.

Industrial zones have several positive effects in the SimCity model, but there is a negative effect that should be emphasized. Because industrial zones contribute to pollution, and pollution subsequently reduces land value, causing migration and reduced population, it is a good idea to segregate the manufacturing areas of your city from the residential areas.

Urban Jungle:
Population Density

High levels of population density tend to signal increases in the crime rate, overcrowding, and slum conditions. Many urban planners insist that this does not have to be the case. Indeed, Tokyo has a much higher population density than New York City with only around ten percent of the crime. Nevertheless, SimCity generalizes this factor and posits a direct relationship between rising population density and increasing crime. It is possible, however, to apply some of the lessons taught by urban planners to your city and reduce the negative effects of high population density.

Many people confuse a concentration of population with overcrowding and poverty. As the visionary Le Corbusier observed, concentration does not have to equal congestion. His perspective was that high-density apartment buildings and office spaces would allow for surrounding open spaces, which could enhance the quality of life.

If one can guarantee that open space will be available for public use as compensation for high-rise buildings, Le Corbusier is probably correct. In modern America, however, territory that would ideally be alloted for open space tends to be usurped by other urban demands. In particular, housing that can support roughly 400 persons per acre requires a parking structure large enough to devour space that could otherwise be utilized for gardens, patios, and playgrounds. An office building that holds 1,200 persons per acre would require a three- or four-story parking garage where one would prefer a park. "The 'green' space to which we aspire and which offers much promise," observe Gallion and Eisner, in *The Urban Pattern: City Planning and Design,* "actually becomes a pavement for the vehicles of transportation."

Fortunately, the SimCity player can be somewhat more successful in alternating green belts with high concentrations of population than most urban planners. The SimCity model does not require you to build parking structures. Therefore, you do not have to bulldoze any terrain other than that which is needed to develop the residential zone itself. This means that you can conserve an incredible amount of available forest and shoreline. Because forests and shorelines add to land value and a higher land value reduces crime, building residential areas next to open spaces limits some of the negatives created by high population density. Because planting parks also adds to land value, an aggressive park building campaign can reduce some of the negative factors associated with high-density population centers.

Another way to slow the growth of the crime rate is to strategically place new police departments. Placing a police department in a high population density area does directly reduce the crime rate, but it does *not* directly increase the land value and cause a corresponding increase in the amount of taxes collected. By lowering the crime rate, it *indirectly* raises land values and enhances the taxes collected. Generally speaking, however, new police precincts add to the expense side of the city ledger.

Alert SimCity players have also noted that *redevelopment* does not work. When land value drops significantly in one of your city's zones, the terrain tiles that depict the buildings in that zone will begin to show decay. My initial impression was that the buildings simply needed demolishing so that new buildings could be constructed. This doesn't work.

When buildings start to decay in SimCity, this is not a function of the buildings themselves. It has nothing to do with the type of buildings in the zone. It is a result of the land value function. This discussion brings to mind the misguided warning posted on a BBS by a novice player: "Watch out for low-valued churches!" as though it were the church bringing the zone down. Instead, it was the land value in the zone bringing the church's value down (unintentionally representative of vandalism, perhaps?).

Therefore, you must solve inner city decay by working on the surrounding problems, rather than attempting a simple, but ineffective, redevelopment program. You must reduce pollution, crime, population density, traffic, and economic stagnation if you wish to revive the values of these zones. As in real life, government-subsidized housing will not accomplish enough if the root cause of an area's problem is, for example, unemployment.

Pop! Go the People!: Important Calculations

The final topic of this chapter concerns how the calculations related to population fit together with the changes in your city. First, note that every zone on the map is periodically updated as the EvalPop (evaluate population) function is called. Second, pay attention to the spiral effect in which higher crime and higher population density lead to lower land value. When these factors are updated, the lower land value can cause further ripple effects in your city's economy.

CHAPTER 4
HEAVY TRAFFIC

When Will Wright, the creator of SimCity, was asked to describe the most realistic aspect of the game, he proudly pointed to the traffic density model. He noted that urban planners regularly identify this function as the most impressive part of the SimCity algorithm and that the routines for this part of the program are the most complex. In fact, the traffic model is so recursive that it takes up 30 percent of your computer's CPU (Central Processing Unit) time to perform the calculations necessary to update the game. In view of the fact that the entire SimCity simulation takes up only 50 percent of your computer's CPU time during most of the game (the animated tile sequences take up the rest), this is an impressive amount of detail.

One reason that many urban planners like the traffic density model in SimCity is that it seems to be a no-win situation, just like it is in real life. Indeed, if you have come to believe (like many people who live in metropolitan areas) that traffic expands to fill the roads and freeways allotted, you will find SimCity to be very realistic.

Spontaneous Generation: The Traffic Phenomenon

In the United States, there is a statistical basis for the thesis that traffic expands to fill the number of lanes allotted. Figure 4-1 shows a chart compiled by Nebojsa Nakicenovic, in "U.S. Transport Infrastructures," that demonstrates the definitive correlation between the increase in total numbers of cars in the U.S. and the substitution of surfaced roads for unpaved roads. Nakicenovic notes that aggregate road mileage has not changed significantly in this century, increasing only about one quarter of a million total miles. A more significant factor has been the replacement of unpaved roads with paved roads. This phenomenon made it more reasonable for Americans to purchase motor vehicles and caused a commensurate inflation in the number of automobiles in use, compared to the number of horse-powered vehicles.

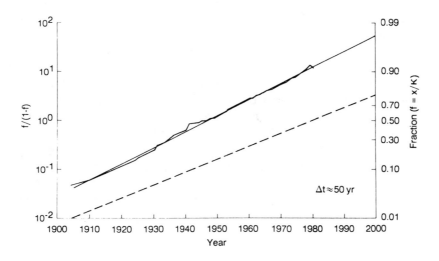

Figure 4-1.   Relationship between surfaced roads and growth in number of motor vehicles in the U.S. (dashed line represents vehicles, solid line represents mileage of surfaced roads)

For example, there were less than 80,000 motorcars in use during 1905 when only 8 percent of all roads were surfaced, but about 3.3 million horses were in use strictly for transportation, with around 22 million draft animals used primarily for farming purposes. By 1920, when there were approximately 500,000 miles of paved road, there were more than 2 million cars being utilized and nearly the same number of horses used strictly for transportation.

In the early 1930s, it was widely believed that the number of automobiles in the U.S. had reached the saturation point. However, massive public works programs for highway construction, which were implemented to combat the effects of the depression during the latter years of that decade, set off more upward momentum in automobile ownership (see Figure 4-2). At the present time, Nakicenovic anticipates that the aggregate number of automobiles owned and operated in the U.S. will reach its saturation point by approximately A.D. 2040.

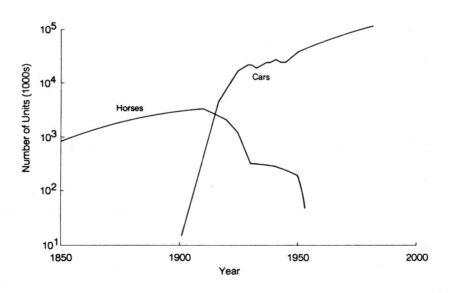

Figure 4-2.   *Comparison of transportation animals versus motor vehicles (note the flattening of the growth trend in the early 1930s)*

Give My Regard to Broad Ways: A Wrong Answer

Even a casual SimCity player will soon learn what urban planners and traffic engineers have been discovering for the last few decades—the strategy of widening existing streets and building new major and secondary highways is not a viable solution to traffic congestion. All of this street widening and major construction simply serves to invite even more traffic onto the expanded street network.

There is an economic irony to the fact that the more you try to plan and build for expanded traffic, the more new traffic will exceed your expectations and capacity. Because each motor vehicle on the road requires at least 4,000 square feet of real estate combined with support structures, Gallion and Eisner, in *The Urban Pattern: City Planning and Design*, have estimated that it costs in excess of $5,000 per year in *land rent* to use one car. This land rent is exacted through consumer prices, which cover the overhead for parking lots and structures in commercial zones (shopping centers, professional offices, and recreational facilities), and through higher mortgage and rent payments for garages and parking lots in residential zones.

The sad reality of this economic "catch 22" was noted by Harrison Salisbury, a *New York Times* reporter who is extensively quoted in Jane Jacobs' *The Death and Life of Great American Cities*. Salisbury states that, "...as more and more space is allotted to the automobile, the goose that lays the golden eggs is strangled." He observes that each widened street and each new road takes more potentially useful land off the tax rolls and starts to cost the government in upkeep, law enforcement, and emergency services.

SimCity will teach you this lesson very quickly. For example, one solution to traffic problems that inexperienced players will often choose is simply to build additional roads. As in real life, this does not work, and traffic expands to meet the capacity of the new road network. If you choose this particular strategy, you will find that you not only end up with considerably more traffic density, but that the cost of maintaining your new roads will be added immediately into your transportation department's budget for next year. You not only fail to solve the problem, but you end up with more expenses. Particularly when playing the Bern (Switzerland) scenario, you will discover that you cannot afford to lose any of your tax base. Even playing in the Easy mode, the default spending deficit in the initial city budget will break you within seven years if you don't find more substantial solutions to the traffic crisis than building new streets and highways (both of which are called "roads," of course, in SimCity).

The Haussmann of the Opera: Haussmannization

One important lesson with regard to traffic engineering can be learned from the redevelopment of Paris beginning in 1853. At that time, Baron Georges-Eugene Haussmann was selected by Napoleon III to administer and organize a plan to completely renew and revitalize the central city of Paris. For a period of seventeen years, Baron Haussmann was given a free hand to develop and implement a plan in which his conceptions of order, convenience, variety, and grandeur could be realized, regardless of expense. The father of the enormous boulevards of Paris (see Figure 4-3) and of monumental public works such as the famous Opera of Paris and Les Halles—the central marketplace of Paris until the late 1960s—Haussmann has been both eulogized as a man of vision and denounced as a ruthless instrument of his emperor.

Even though some of his policies do not greatly help with modern traffic congestion (for reasons already cited in the preceding section), certain of his concepts are still important. While widening streets doesn't solve congestion in today's world, Haussmann's wide boulevards accomplished three tasks. First, they permitted troops and artillery to move easily through the city in order to quell any public insurrections. Second, cutting the large avenues through the foul and congested labyrinths of the inner city improved sanitation by making light and fresh air more accessible to apartments and archaic narrow courts. Third, and most important for modern planners, he demonstrated how advantageous it can be to remove bottlenecks and provide for more efficient circulation of traffic, a process known as *Haussmannization.*

Le Corbusier was tremendously influenced by Haussmann's policy of straightening Parisian boulevards. In *The City of To-Morrow and its Planning,* he writes: "The circulation of traffic demands the straight

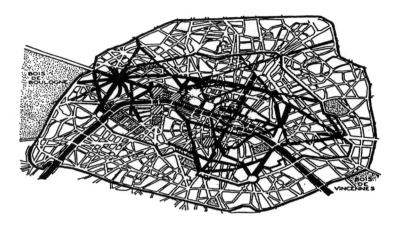

Figure 4-3.   Haussmann's redevelopment of Paris (note that the shaded roads represent those that Haussmann straightened)

line; it is the proper thing for the heart of a city." He goes on to observe that curves have a tendency to paralyze the circulation of traffic and recounts an anecdote about an automobile ride with a representative of a German Chamber of Commerce. Noting that the businessman slowed down when he came to winding sections of road and delightedly accelerated as he came to straight sections, Le Corbusier insisted that it is essential that automobiles be allowed to travel as directly as possible.

Uncorking Bottlenecks: A Partial Answer

In SimCity, there is a useful application of Haussmannization. Just as curves, bridges, and intersections tend to slow traffic in reality, so do curves, bridges, and intersections in SimCity. Particularly in the Bern scenario, there are several bridges that are awkward to approach because of sharp curves just before them, as well as an automobile bridge with limited capacity (see Figure 4-4). Whenever possible, it is a good

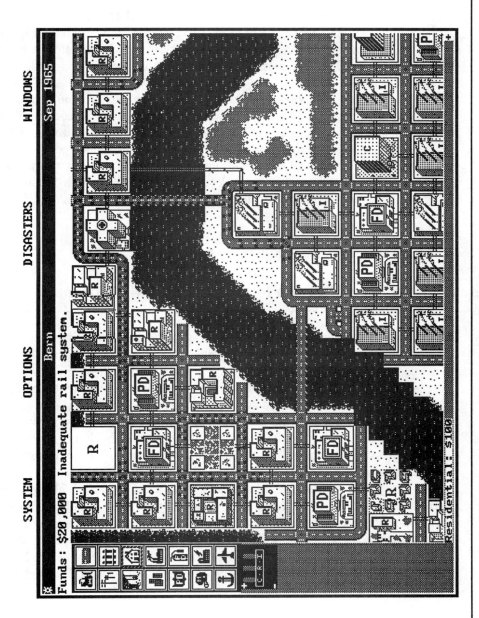

Figure 4-4. Typical bottleneck near bridgeheads (Bern scenario)

idea to bulldoze and rezone the area immediately adjacent to the bridge, as well as the bridge and roadway themselves, so that you can construct a straight rail line with much higher passenger capacity (see Figure 4-5). This is an important part of the equation for winning in the Bern scenario and will often help you straighten out traffic congestion in other scenarios.

Some will undoubtedly argue that straightening streets and roads to improve efficiency is a bankrupt process that causes entire communities to be locked into a faceless gridiron pattern. For a time, planners went to curvilinear designs in order to give the community more personality, but it is ironic that these attempts tended to devolve into "curved grids" (according to Gallion and Eisner). You will find that there is no advantage to using unnecessary curves in road or rail designs in SimCity.

The SimCity School of Modeling: Traffic Calculations

In real life, planners figure that an average city street with intersections placed at a normal distance from each other will allow roughly 700 to 800 passenger cars per lane to pass a given point in an hour. The same street will accommodate around 180 buses per lane per hour (according to Gallion and Eisner). Because studies have shown that the average passenger car will carry 1.5 persons per car, but buses carry anywhere from 42 to 60 persons (82 for most double-deckers), the same street can handle passenger traffic from a low of 1,200 people per hour (private vehicles only) to a high of 7,200 people (buses only).

When you consider that the typical freeway can carry 1,500 private automobiles in the same hour (2,500 passengers), but a rail line using the same right of way could carry 27,000 passengers in the same hour (Gallion and Eisner), you will understand why SimCity's model favors the use of light rail. (For some objections to the simplicity of the light rail model, see the section of this chapter entitled, "Don't Rail On My Parade: Rail Problems.")

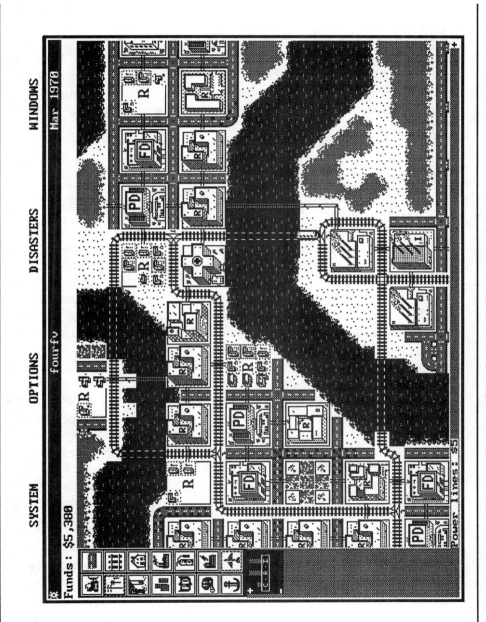

Figure 4-5. Light rail line used to straighten bottleneck (Bern scenario)

In order to determine the most efficient transportation network for a given area, planners need to have some idea of the number of trips generated from a given zone to a given zone. In "Transport," David Briggs discusses how, at one time, door-to-door surveys were conducted in various housing developments to determine the trip patterns in a given zone (t_{ij}). Then future needs were forecast by multiplying an expected growth factor (E) times t_{ij} to get the total number of future trips T_{ij}.

Unfortunately, the values utilized to derive E often turned out to be too arbitrary to be of much use. Therefore, a more involved calculation was devised. In this case the formula is

$$T_{ij} = A_i B_j O_i D_j f(d_{ij})$$

O_i represents the number of trips that originate in zone i, multiplied by D_j (the number of trips attracted to zone j), A_i (the attractiveness of zone i), B_j (the attractiveness of zone j), and a factor that reflects the travel time between the zones (d_{ij}). Even more complex formulae are available to attempt to determine the traffic distribution of an area, but none of them accomplish much without consideration of land use zones (Briggs).

Transportation planning requires careful integration with plans for land use zones. In SimCity, there is a basic formula like the one presented in the preceding paragraph for each type of land use zone. In one formula, a residential zone is the origin zone, while nearby commercial or industrial zones are the destination. In another formula, a commercial zone is the origin zone, while residential and industrial zones are the destination. A third formula has an industrial zone as the point of origin, while residential zones (evidently representing the commute home) are the destination. In all three formulae, the trip range is modified by traffic density (which is similar to the trip duration factor in the formula given in the preceding paragraph).

The SimCity approach is not very different from that used by decision-makers in real life. Recently, Twentieth Century Fox was attempting to gain approval to build new offices and production facilities on the site of its old Century City movie lot. The company's television network had increased its need for production facilities to such an extent that it decided to revitalize the lot.

The problem, which has not been solved as of this writing, is that during a period of dormant film production, the company had managed to get the Century City lot rezoned for high-rise condominium development. They had intended to sell off large portions of the property. Naturally, the studio's neighbors fought the condominium development quite fiercely. They didn't want the additional traffic flow. At the present time, they are fighting the attempt to get the studio property rezoned once more, because they believe that production facilities (equivalent to SimCity's industrial zones) and offices (equivalent to SimCity's commercial zones) will generate more trips than condominiums (equivalent to SimCity's residential zones).

Not Doing a Slow Bern: Land Use Considerations

When you boot SimCity, you are given the option of choosing a scenario. The scenarios provide the basic data for managing a specific city during a specific time frame. Each scenario features a different overall problem and gives you a limited amount of time to solve the problem. The Bern, Switzerland scenario deals with the traffic congestion in 1965. In order to win at this simple scenario, you are given ten years to reach low average traffic density throughout the city. If you succeed, you receive the "Key to the City," a victory screen to celebrate your achievement (see Figure 4-6).

One of the major problems for many who play the Bern scenario is that they lose sight of the overall picture. They realize that there are significant traffic problems, so they move to solve those without considering the additional problems faced by the simulated city. Initially, the city has a tremendous problem with deficit spending. You must not only solve the traffic snarls, but you must do something to reduce the drain on the municipal budget as well.

Here is where the integration of land use with traffic planning offers considerable value. Even creating a roadless city and substituting rails for every block of road (if you had the funds) would not solve many of

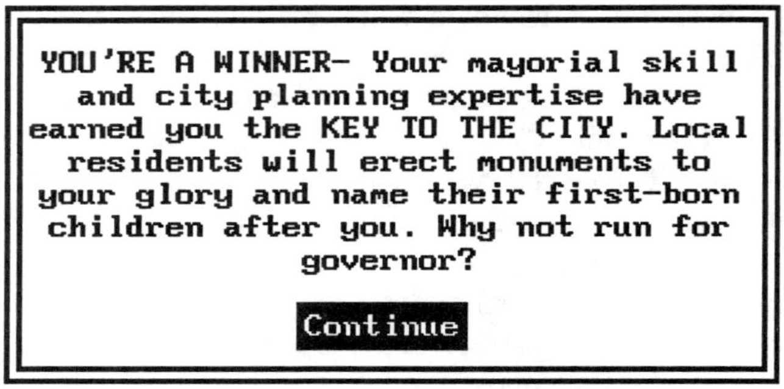

```
YOU'RE A WINNER- Your mayorial skill
    and city planning expertise have
earned you the KEY TO THE CITY. Local
    residents will erect monuments to
your glory and name their first-born
children after you. Why not run for
                 governor?

                Continue
```

Figure 4-6.   Victory screen for SimCity scenarios

these problems. Simply substituting rails for roads is as ridiculous as dreaming of purely pedestrian cities, the nostalgic days of horse-drawn transportation, or a metropolis dependent on bicycle traffic.

In the case of the bicycle and horse-drawn alternatives, Jacobs notes in *The Death and Life of Great American Cities* that horses caused just as much congestion (as well as their own type of pollution) in the past, and that "...people who have experienced an Amsterdam or New Delhi rush hour report that bicycles in massive numbers become an appalling mixture with pedestrians...."

Don't Rail on My Parade: Rail Problems

In the case of the roadless city, science fiction author and technological gadfly Jerry Pournelle rather brutally castigated SimCity's predilection for light rail solutions in a column in *Byte* magazine, in which he noted that it would be possible to build a roadless city, but "...such a city would soon strangle in garbage." This is a colorful way of noting that we need point-to-point transportation for certain public services. One must imagine a garbage train, a delivery train, a fire-fighting train, and a law enforcement train in order to comprehend a roadless city.

In SimCity, you must work with what the model gives you, and the only way to really solve the transportation problem includes building a light rail network. You are fortunate not to have to worry about scheduling trains, building stations, providing parking, or developing a fare structure in order to accomplish this. You simply bulldoze the existing roads and replace them with rails. However, there is an important consideration. When you substitute the rails for roads, you want to create a transportation network that fits your municipal budget.

Satellite Development: A Partial Solution

With budgetary considerations in mind, there are two open areas in the SimCity map of Bern that would be conducive to expanded development. To the northeast, you can establish a string of industrial zones located immediately to the north of the power plants and buttressed against the eastern boundary of the map. This enables you to avoid 50 percent of the polluting effects of this heavy industrial zone and offers a potentially significant increase in the tax base.

Of course, you have to zone some residential areas where the workers for those industrial zones will live and a couple of commercial zones for them to shop in. The key to the success of this venture is that the satellite city be self-contained in terms of transportation. You build rail lines from the residential zones to the commercial and industrial zones, but do not necessarily connect these lines to the rest of the city until you are ready to start your Haussmannization program (Figure 4-7).

Another option is to immediately bulldoze all of the excess roads on the western side of the map of Bern (Figure 4-8). There are miles and miles of road, which cost a significant amount of the transportation department's budget, but do not serve a useful purpose, since it is not practical to zone and develop the properties where these roads are located. If you should decide to develop the section of land where these roads are located, you will find that you exacerbate the traffic problems.

If you bulldoze the roads on the west side, you immediately accomplish two things. First, you reduce the city's current expenses by reducing the transportation budget. Second, you offer yourself the opportunity to create a satellite on the west side like the one I suggested building on the east side. If you position the new zones and rail lines so that they line up squarely with the major roads in the downtown areas of Bern, you will be in a very good position to bulldoze through the

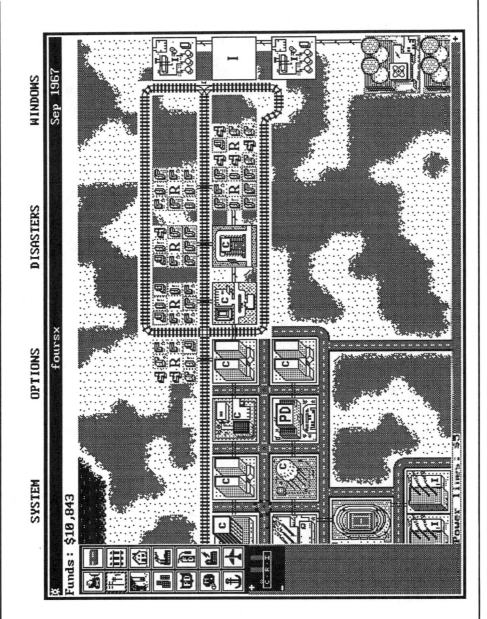

Figure 4-7.   Establishing a satellite development to increase Bern's tax base

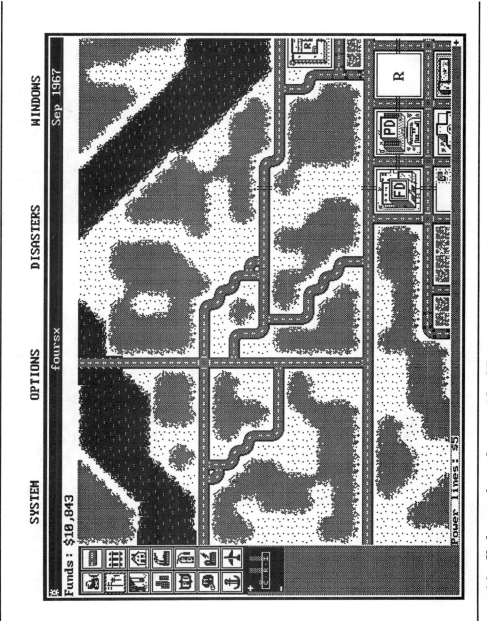

Figure 4-8. Useless roads on the west side of Bern

central city and establish a light rail line, which could feasibly solve the traffic density problem.

Picking the Public Pocket: Financial Wizardry

In addition to these legitimate strategies, there are two rather wicked ways to avoid the financial constraints of the scenarios. First, you can reduce the fire department's and police department's budgets to 50 percent or less. You will have to raise the police department's budget when the citizens begin to complain about rising crime rates, but the fire department can be exploited until a disaster occurs. You are essentially gambling with the lives of your citizens, but it offers advantages without affecting the score too much.

Second, you can use the *embezzling function*. After all, real cities, counties, and states do this, but they call it a bond issue. Don't use the embezzling function too much, however, because the program discourages this by causing an earthquake to occur, even if you've toggled off all the disasters.

IBM   On the IBM and compatibles, simply hold down the SHIFT key and type **FUND**, and $10,000 will be added to your city's operating funds.

Amiga and Macintosh   On the Amiga and Macintosh, you must hold down the SHIFT key, type **FUND**, and click the mouse button on the Bulldozer icon.

C-64/128   On the C-64/128, you can change your current fund status to $4,000 by pressing the F1 key. The bad news is that it changes your status to $4,000 no matter how much you have before you press the key, but since an airport costs only $4,000 in the C-64/128 version, and that's the most expensive project in the program, it shouldn't hurt you. The good news is that the C-64/128 version doesn't call up the earthquake, no matter how many times you press F1.

Hardening of the Arteries: Conclusions

Traffic is much like your body's circulatory system. You cannot live
without it because that would mean the total removal of critical resources (that is, the work force, food, supplies in raw and manufactured
form, conveniences, and services). In this chapter, you should have
learned not to build roads and rails that you do not need. Not only does
traffic expand to fill the roads allotted, but each road potentially takes
away from more profitable use of the land. You should also have observed the necessity of removing bottlenecks (in order to reduce trip
distance between destinations) and discovered some of the principles
underlying the traffic algorithms used in SimCity. The management of
urban traffic requires carefully integrated planning, taking into consideration the transportation network itself and the zones it connects, in
order to create a smoothly functioning environment.

CHAPTER 5
ECOLOGY AND ENTROPY

In many ways, modern urban life makes the average citizen feel like he or she is in the middle of that giant trash compactor in the original *Star Wars* film. We have toxic waste oozing out of the ground and into underground water tables. Our eyes burn from noxious smog, and our lungs fight to transform that same smog into a breathable substance. The struggle looks hopeless, but the human spirit seeks solutions nevertheless.

This chapter quickly summarizes some of the ecological problems facing modern cities and explains how SimCity models these problems. It then describes ways of dealing with these problems, with particular attention to the Boston and Detroit scenarios. SimCity does not deal with ecological crises like soil erosion (nearly one-third of United States farmland—50 million hectares—is undergoing a significant decline in long-term productivity due to soil erosion), shrinking rain forests (aggregate global coverage dropped from 15 percent to 12 percent between 1950 and 1975), marine pollution (oceans are currently accepting harmful chemicals at the following multipliers times the normal rate: mercury

(2.5), manganese (4), zinc (12), copper (12), antimony (30), and phospho-rus (80)), acidification of the atmosphere (in certain parts of Pennsylva-nia, during the 1980s, the acid content of rain reached a level more than 1,000 times greater than the amount found in natural rain), and contam-ination of ground water (more than 80 percent of the diseases that affect the so-called Third World are transmitted by impure water). Instead, SimCity focuses strictly on the relationship of air pollution to quality of life and on the trade-offs involved in the choice between nuclear-powered and more traditional coal-powered plants. Indeed, you will find yourself trying to decide whether you should risk the deaths of thou-sands of people and potential contamination of thousands of acres of developed property in order to save operating costs in the short run or gradually pollute the atmosphere over a longer period of time in order to play it relatively safe.

To Air Is Human: Air Quality

Contrary to the opinion of a former presidential candidate, who claimed that trees were a primary source of pollution, the two major polluters of urban air are heavy industry and the automobile. Every year, more than 450,000 tons of lead are released into the atmosphere from these two sources, whereas only 3,500 tons are released by natural sources. The catalytic action of sunlight on a mixture of hydrocarbons and nitrogen oxides creates a multitude of problems for the urban dweller.

The *Los Angeles Times* prints a daily summary of atmospheric quality, which measures the following irritants: ozone (invisible mole-cules that irritate the lungs and reduce the effectiveness of breathing), nitrogen dioxide (molecules that join together to form a visible brown cloud and impair breathing), carbon monoxide (an invisible compound that reduces the blood's oxygen content), and micron particulates (which affect the lungs on a deep level and reduce atmospheric visibility). A Pollutant Standard Index (PSI) is utilized to indicate the average pene-tration of pollutants (ranging on a scale from 0 to 275+ to reflect a spectrum from good to hazardous). In SimCity, you can get an idea of your city's PSI by using the Pollution map to track the highest concen-trations of pollution.

You can test the causal relationship of traffic and industry to pollution by loading a city with heavy concentrations of traffic and industry. Then, using the Pollution map, identify the highest concentration of air pollution. Now it's time to do what every mayor has probably dreamed of at one time or another. Return to the Edit Window and click on the Bulldozer icon. Point the cursor at the offending area and reduce it to clear terrain. Let the simulation run for about six months and return to the Pollution map. Pollution should be considerably reduced.

Of course, the answers to such a complex problem are never that simple. As discussed in the last chapter, rapid transit can be part of the solution, but a much more integrated approach to city planning can be more effective.

In Fort Worth, Texas, Victor Gruen and Associates attempted to solve the problem with a radical proposal for surrounding the central city area with a ring road along the circumference of the business district (see Figure 5-1). A series of multistory garages would be placed at intervals along this ring road, and the interiors of these garages would project into the central city itself. The roads in the central portion of the city would be closed to vehicular traffic, but the distances from the interiors of these garages to locations in the center of the city would not be too great. A series of underground service tunnels would allow delivery and service vehicles access to downtown locations via service elevators. Taxis would deliver out-of-town visitors to the downtown hotels via the underground routes and special elevators, as well.

The plan was stalled because of political opposition, but the benefits of such an arrangement are, at best, unproven. Would the garages actually accommodate the numbers of vehicles required to staff the central city and allow entrance and exit by the business, shopping, and tourist population? Would such an artificial line of demarcation between vehicular and pedestrian traffic actually encourage responsible downtown development and growth, or would it simply freeze the city's center out of the normal flow of life (that is, would the city center become so inconvenient that no one would bother to go there)?

You can simulate the effect of the Gruen plan when you develop residential areas in SimCity. In order to accommodate optimal population growth without creating severe pollution, many players like to create strips of residential zones in 2 x 6 plots with a ring road surrounding each one. This has the effect of providing vehicular access to all of the zones in the strip, without excess roads and their inevitable

Figure 5-1.   The Gruen Plan (courtesy of Gruen Associates)

high traffic density and high pollution levels. In addition, it is probably a good idea to put a police department in every other strip, alternating with fire departments. This is potentially costly, so be certain that your overall city budget can handle the additional maintenance costs.

Note, however, that the same strategy that seems to work so well with residential zones will virtually assure strips of high pollution and dense traffic in commercial and industrial zones. The best antipollution strategy with regard to industrial zones is to separate them from each other and leave open space between them. Ideally, the open space should include some forested areas or parks, which would improve air quality by using up some of the carbon dioxide in the air. SimCity does not directly figure this effect into the model, however. Rather, as noted in Chapter 3, the effect of natural (passive) or planned (active) open space, such as parks, is to add to the land value.

Deadweight in Detroit: Tips on Winning

Although ecological concerns are not the only ones at work in the Detroit 1972 scenario, they are certainly a good place to begin. The city begins in financial disaster, and it needs radical surgery on the budget before any curative measures can be brought forward. The 1973 Fiscal Budget window shown in Figure 5-2 illustrates Detroit's declining economy. The scenario also begins with an inefficient road and rail network. Fortunately, there is a way to address both problems. Roads are expensive to maintain and, as noted in Chapter 4, tend to encourage expanded traffic density, which, in turn, increases air pollution (see Figure 5-3). Therefore, the very first step is to eliminate redundant roads and replace the main roads with light rails. In this way, you will reduce your budget and alleviate some of the major pollutants in one bold move.

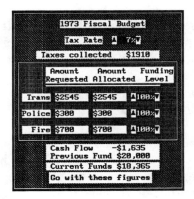

Figure 5-2. A 1973 Fiscal Budget window in the Detroit scenario

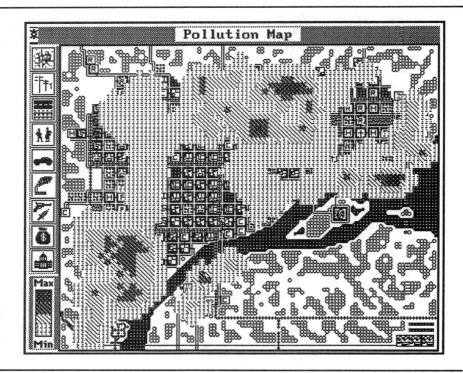

Figure 5-3.   Pollution concentrations in the Detroit scenario

Once you've solved the financial crisis and transformed your negative cash flow into a positive one, it's time for a major redevelopment effort. Should you need to fudge just a bit on your budget, however, note that reducing services to about 75 percent across the board is a quick and dirty way to change cash flow. You'll have to do some repairs on the transportation infrastructure in the future, but it's usually a way to come out ahead.

Another major problem that you will face in the Detroit scenario is the high crime rate. At the beginning of the scenario, as you will immediately note, there are not enough police stations to stem the tide, as shown in Figure 5-4. It is a good idea to add a couple of police stations during the first couple of years. However, it is even more

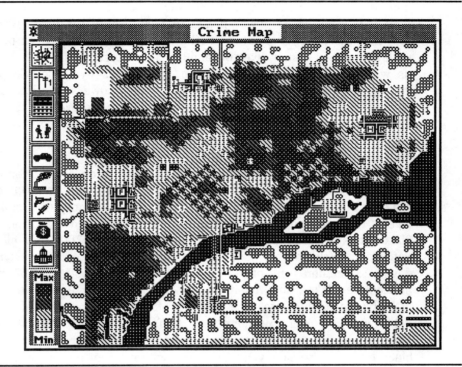

Figure 5-4. Crime concentrations in the Detroit scenario

important to raise the land value as you redevelop the inner city, so be sure to construct some parks in order to create active open space.

The Nuclear Option: Energy Choices

Unfortunately, for those of us who enjoy the realism of SimCity, the energy and pollution options provided in the game are not entirely sufficient. The rate of nuclear accidents, as noted in Chapter 1, is handled fairly, but SimCity does not demonstrate all the potential problems with coal-driven power plants. Although SimCity does reflect the fact that these power plants contribute to air pollution, it does not deal with the cost in human lives of mining and processing the coal. Many of us would prefer to use such "clean" options as hydroelectric plants, geothermal conversion of energy, solar energy towers, windmill farms, windmill-bearing balloons in the tropopause, and photovoltaic cells. This doesn't include more novel experiments like converting garbage into energy or transforming coconut waste into electricity. Alas, such options do not exist in SimCity.

What you do get in SimCity is a choice between coal-powered and nuclear-powered electricity. The burning of coal to produce electricity is a messy business that contributes significantly to atmospheric pollution. Every 1,000 megawatts of electricity created adds to the atmosphere 65,000 tons of sulfur dioxide (an acidic compound), 25,000 tons of nitrogen dioxide (the brown substance that you see in the air on smoggy days), 1.6 million tons of carbon dioxide, and 120,000 tons of micron particulates. It's a dirty business and SimCity lets you get away with a little bit as it calculates the pollution from these plants. Add to the debits of coal-burning power plants the fact that around 70 coal miners annually die in accidents worldwide and the fact that many more die of black lung disease each year. You can easily see that power produced by coal is a costly option.

On the other hand, nuclear-powered facilities would seem to be clean burning, pollution free sources of energy. The power companies that have invested in this technology would have us believe that nuclear power plants pose little risk. They tell us this despite the construction of reactors near off-shore faults and despite the fact that we have yet to discover a reasonably safe way to dispose of nuclear waste. We are given political slogans on bumper stickers designed to convince us that those who are concerned about nuclear safety are ignorant extremists.

Pronuclear activists treat the Chernobyl disaster as an aberration and point to decades of trouble-free nuclear operation in order to advocate further growth in the nuclear power industry. Awareness of the history of nuclear power can effectively undermine this certainty. In 1957 a reactor fire in the United Kingdom contaminated more than 750 square kilometers of land. In 1976 there was a radioactive leak of more than two million liters near the same site. In 1981 milk supplies in the same area were contaminated by a release of iodine 131, a radioactive element with a mercifully short half-life of eight days (that is, it loses half its potency in eight days, three-fourths by sixteen days, and so forth).

Britain is not the only nation to be so affected. In 1958 the Soviet Union was disposing of nuclear waste in the Ural Mountains when the waste site exploded and killed hundreds of people. In 1968 a reactor near Detroit had to be shut down because part of the core of a fast breeder reactor overheated and began to melt. In 1969 the operators of a Colorado waste pile reported that spontaneous ignition caused a release of plutonium dust. In 1972, a New York plant specializing in plutonium handling was permanently closed following an explosion. In 1975, at Brown's Ferry, Alabama, a candle started a fire that ended up short-circuiting five emergency systems and nearly destroying the reactor. In 1979, operator error at Three Mile Island, Pennsylvania, led to an accident that destroyed a one-billion-dollar reactor.

When one considers that pollution from nuclear sources has the potential to last thousands of years (plutonium 239's half-life is 24,000 years) or even millions of years (uranium 238's half-life is 4.5 million years) beyond our lifetimes, the decision no longer seems cut and dried. You find yourself weighing the known reality of pollution generated in coal-powered energy production versus the unknown quantity of how long you can avert disaster with a "clean" nuclear power plant.

For most game players, the choice is simple. You will get much more efficiency out of a nuclear power plant, you will not have to fight air pollutants from a nuclear plant, and you can be sure it will not melt down if you replace it every 75 years or so. For those of us who like to play the game consistently with our ethical and political stand, however, the choice is not so simple. Do you deal with the "devil" you know, or do you risk the future of the planet? For me, this question is so nagging, personal, and profound that the only time nuclear power plants show up on my computer screen is when they are already present in a scenario.

The China "Sim"drome: The Boston 2010 Scenario

In the Boston 2010 scenario, you are facing the imminent meltdown of one of your nuclear reactors. The entire scenario lasts only five simu-

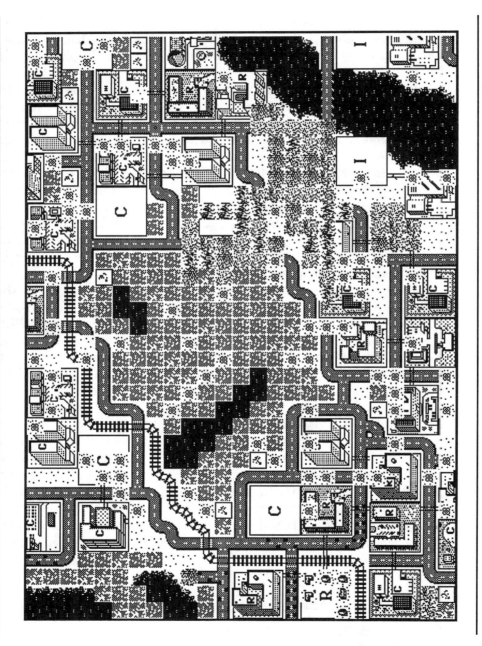

Figure 5-5.   A contaminated area in the Boston scenario

lated years, so you need to find out immediately where all of the nuclear reactors are in relation to other landmarks in the city. This will enable you to restore the power grid to the uncontaminated areas of the city immediately after the meltdown. Then you will know approximately how far to bulldoze down the roads, rails, and buildings within the contaminated area. Figure 5-5 shows a contaminated area of the city that needs to be bulldozed.

In actuality, you wouldn't be sending crews into the contaminated area in order to bulldoze buildings and destroy the existing transportation network. Within the constraints of SimCity, however, you will need to do this for several reasons. First, your transportation budget is charged for every section of rail and road. Therefore, your budget will bleed red ink if you do not complete the wholesale bulldozing. Second, the model will charge the inefficiency of interrupted services and a disrupted transportation network against the quality of life quotient, unless you return this area to barrenness. You have to bulldoze so that your score will not be reduced by a factor that you can no longer control.

Once you have neutralized the effects of the meltdown by isolating this section of the city, you proceed as usual. Use the maps to track the problems listed in the city evaluation report, and use the techniques already discussed in this book to solve specific problems. In this way, you should easily be able to keep your overall score for the scenario above 500 and win the Key to the City.

CHAPTER 6
CRASH LANDING

"This has been a test of the Emergency Broadcast System. Had this been an actual emergency . . . ." How many times has your radio listening or television viewing been interrupted by that familiar public service spot? It is deeply ingrained in our culture, and most of us grew up with that nagging reminder of potential disaster gnawing at our psyches. For many of us, however, disaster is the farthest thing from our conscious minds.

This chapter serves two basic purposes. First, it should remind you that nearly every government body has contingency plans for every conceivable emergency. Second, it will offer some techniques for dealing with SimCity scenarios that include disasters.

Perhaps the most ironic fact about disaster preparedness is that local government, the institution most capable of preventing potentially hazardous development, is in fact an entity that has a considerable amount to gain by granting permission to develop borderline properties (those subject to liquefaction and mud slides, and those located on edges of fault lines and flood planes). Local governments often can profit enormously by allowing risky ventures to expand their tax base, no matter how temporary the increase in revenues may be.

On the Boardwalk: Seashore and Flood Plain Development

It often seems that the areas most attractive to new development are precisely those areas that are most dangerous to life and property. Hillside and cliff homes, which are susceptible to mud slides, seaside homes, which could be subject to the ravages of high tides or hurricanes, and riverfront and flood plain homes, which find themselves caught in a recurring build-destroy-rebuild cycle, are only a few examples of this "value in spite of hazard" phenomenon.

It would seem, then, that the most efficient preventive method of dealing with flood and tidal disasters would be to zone potential disaster areas in such a way that development within them would be very limited. This, of course, would be an extremely unpopular policy, and it would be difficult to enforce. A more feasible, but still distinctly unpopular, suggestion was made in a recent work entitled *Catastrophic Coastal Storms: Hazard Mitigation and Development Management,* by Godschalk, Brower, and Beatley. The authors suggest a strict limitation on government disaster relief in areas that are habitually subject to floods and hurricanes. They note that coastal disasters, in particular, are recurring events rather than random catastrophes. Therefore, they plead for government agencies to stop offering the equivalent of public subsidies for the private purpose of rebuilding in hazardous areas.

They suggest that public funds be utilized instead to purchase these hazardous areas, for two reasons. First, the hazardous areas can be zoned in such a way that no "at risk" structures can be developed within them, saving money in disaster relief for the long run. Second, the areas so zoned and purchased can provide much needed open space or beach access areas to serve the public good. Combining these two emphases should make the policy more politically feasible. Similar plans have been put into effect in earthquake sensitive areas, and these will be discussed in the section called "Whole Lotta' Shakin' Goin' On: Earthquakes."

Drain It in Rio: Preventing Floods (Rio de Janeiro)

In actual practice, there are several methods that urban planners use to combat flood and tidal damage. For handling generic flood damage, particularly during the last 50 to 60 years, the establishment of flood control districts with networks of canals, reservoirs, and dams has had tremendous impact on the ability of the United States to cope with flood damage. In addition, coastal and riverfront areas have experimented increasingly with the construction of seawalls, floodproofing of individual buildings, and development of local community evacuation plans. Unfortunately, you do not have these options when playing SimCity. Instead, you will have to opt for a preventive program of land-use restrictions to solve the problems.

To test your prowess at managing a flood disaster, you should boot your computer and select the Rio de Janeiro scenario (Rio 2047 Flooding). This moderately difficult test of your managerial skills is placed in a hypothetical future which posits that the average global temperature will increase six degrees Fahrenheit by the middle of the twenty-first century. If this temperature increase did in fact occur, it would undoubtedly mean the melting of polar ice caps and a subsequent rise in tidal levels. Because Rio de Janeiro has several low coastal plains, the city would be quite susceptible to a disruptive series of floods.

In order to win in the Rio de Janeiro scenario, you have to maintain the metropolis at at least a score of 500 for ten years. This is relatively simple if you engage in a preventive land-use program from the very beginning of play. You should probably play a couple of game years at the Rio de Janeiro scenario so that you can discover the zones that are likely to be flooded. To give you an idea of the flood damage that can occur, Figures 6-1 and 6-2 show the Rio de Janeiro scenario before and after a flood. This should in no way be considered cheating, because flooding is basically a recurring, rather than a random, disaster. Once you have taken note of the basic flood pattern, it is a simple task to restart the scenario and begin your program of preventive land-use planning.

When you start the scenario, you should immediately solve the power problem by building a new power plant, and you should then begin placing zones in the open area in the southwest part of the city (see Figure 6-3). These new zones will replace those zones that will inevitably be flooded out when the sea level rises. In this way, you will be able to bulldoze the affected zones immediately after the crisis, cut your losses with regard to power and transportation grids, and have new developments in a relatively safe area to replace, with regard to your overall tax base, the established developments that you have lost in the flood.

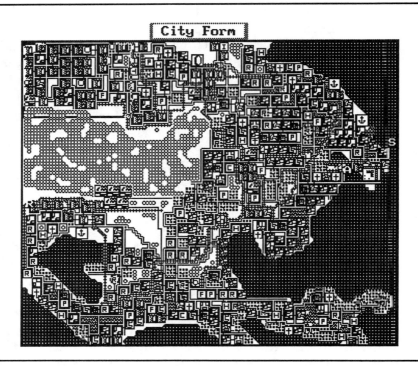

Figure 6-1.   The Rio de Janeiro City Form map before the flooding

If you are so inclined, you can even zone the flood area as parkland, open space, and beach access when the water recedes (by planting parks and leaving the rest open). In this way, you can help to restore property values affected by the flood, keep pollution down by keeping heavy industry out of the area, and keep your score at the level required in order to win the scenario.

Whole Lotta' Shakin' Goin' On: Earthquakes

The image of an earthquake that is most familiar to many of us is the idea of a fissure opening in the crust of the earth like some monstrous

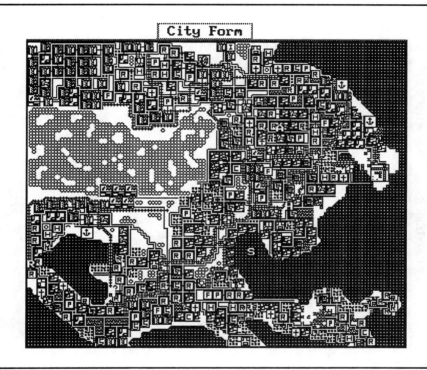

Figure 6-2. *The Rio de Janeiro City Form map after the flooding*

maw ready to devour us. In point of fact, only one animal (a cow that was swallowed up to her tail in the San Francisco quake of 1906) and one human being (a woman in the Fukui, Japan quake of 1948 who was enveloped in a fissure that opened to a width of four feet before it closed over her) ever died in this manner. Indeed, most earthquake-spawned fatalities are caused by buildings collapsing as a result of either structural instability or weak underpinning. The latter can occur as an effect of slope, soil, or fault line.

Because the latter type of earthquake-related death can be minimized by seismic safety planning, many states have been progressively upgrading their requirements as regards both seismic engineering (constructing buildings that can withstand not only vertical, but also lateral and torsional stress) and land-use restrictions. The problem is that

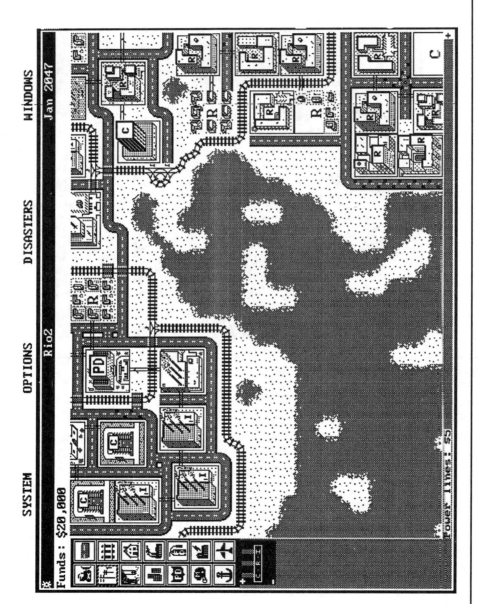

Figure 6-3.   Open space in southwest Rio de Janeiro

earthquakes are rather unpleasant disasters to consider and, according to former California Seismic Safety Commission Chairman George Mader, "...earthquake preparedness is not a popular topic."

It's Not My Fault: Seismic Zoning

In California, mapping of fault lines is a vital part of every local government's master plan, making it easy to comply with the provisions of the 1972 Alquist-Priolo Act, which states that neither public nor private buildings can be situated across the trace of an active fault. Of course, most planning commissions no longer allow buildings anywhere near the fault lines themselves.

Another potential danger related to seismic activity (but not exclusively so) is liquefaction. This is the process in which a cohesionless soil base is, through seismic activity or change in ground water level, temporarily transformed into a fluid mass. Developments built on landfills and alluvium, such as the Marina district of San Francisco, are particularly susceptible to liquefaction. As a result of damage from the October, 1989 earthquake in San Francisco, a full review of plans for construction in the Marina district will take place. This is similar to a study in Seattle, Washington that was prompted by a moderate earthquake in 1965. Seattle and King County, Washington are so concerned about potential earthquake danger that voters approved a $117 million bond issue in 1989 in order to acquire open space areas. In keeping with the dual purpose of meeting the need for open space and restricting the development of earthquake-sensitive zones, much of the acquisition in the Washington bond issue will be in areas that are vulnerable to earthquake damage.

Legislative and planning efforts to restrict land use in particularly hazardous sites is called seismic zoning. It is the primary weapon in preventive disaster planning. Unfortunately, there is no way to determine hazardous sites prior to the earthquakes themselves when you are playing SimCity. Therefore, you will need to prepare your city to recover from damage caused by the earthquake rather than prevent such damage.

We're All Shook Up: San Francisco

One of the most challenging scenarios in SimCity is the challenge of managing San Francisco, California after the 1906 earthquake, which is estimated to have measured over 8.0 on the Richter scale. When you load SimCity, you simply choose the San Francisco 1906 Earthquake scenario. Then, when the city loads, you will have five years of game time not only to rebuild after the earthquake, but to guide the city to the Metropolis level and maintain it at that level. This may be the most challenging set of circumstances that you will face in order to gain the coveted Key to the City, which indicates you have won at SimCity management.

Note that fires and explosions are often in evidence after earthquakes. Figures 6-4 and 6-5 show City Form maps of San Francisco before and after the earthquake. Notice the outbreak of fires in Figure 6-5. An even closer view of the fires is shown in Figure 6-6. In SimCity, your city's future will depend on how well you respond to these immedi-

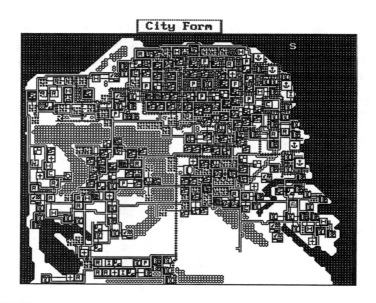

Figure 6-4.   The San Francisco City Form map before the earthquake

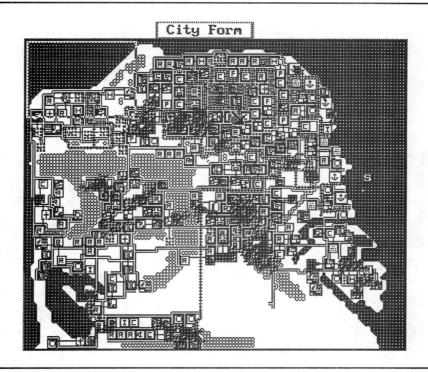

Figure 6-5. *The San Francisco City Form map after the earthquake*

ate postcrisis events. Fortunately, the observant SimCity mayor often has a chance to do some quick preventive maintenance prior to the actual earthquake. In the San Francisco scenario, in particular, there are only five fire departments in the entire city. Figure 6-7 shows San Francisco's inadequate protection against fire. Quick placement of at least one new fire department (preferably two) prior to the quake itself can make a big difference in terms of getting the fires out faster. Because your score is completely dependent on what you can do in five game years, it is extremely important that you get those fires out in a hurry.

Once the Big One hits, you need to be ready for some strong decisive action with the Bulldozer icon. The fastest way to ensure that the fires do not spread is to bulldoze the center of any zone that has a fire in it.

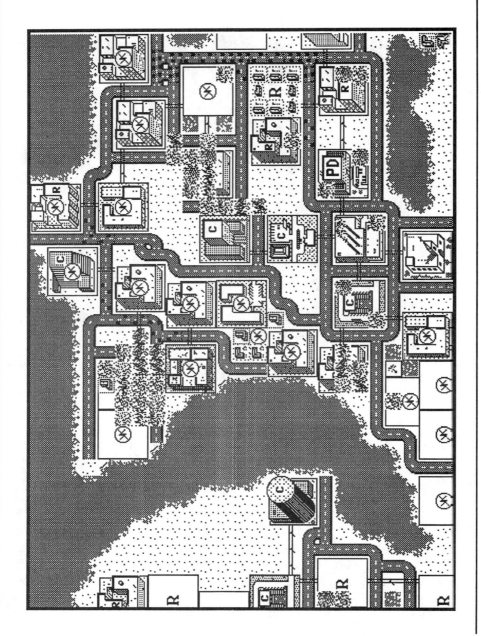

Figure 6-6. Detail of fires caused by the earthquake

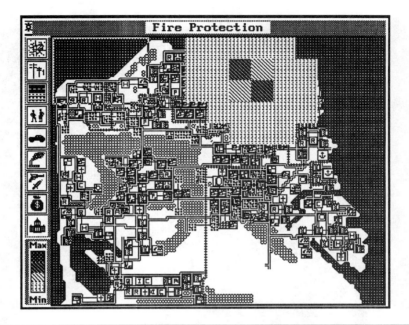

Figure 6-7. The San Francisco Fire Protection Radius map

Then bulldoze rubble, roads, rails, and woods all around the fire so that there is at least one square of clear terrain surrounding the tile that represents the fire. This will ensure that the fire cannot spread. Repeat this procedure for every fire shown on the map. This simulates the best efforts of trained emergency personnel in the hours immediately following a major disaster.

As soon as you neutralize the fire threat, you must restore the power grid. The earthquake, fire, and explosive damage will have created several power outages at various points on the map as shown in Figure 6-8. It is vital that you restore power as soon as possible. When a zone loses power, it does not stop paying taxes, but people move out. The less people, the less taxes; when all the people are gone, there are no taxes. This migration could take a few years, depending on the original population of the zone. You must keep the population up during this scenario if you want to win the Key to the City.

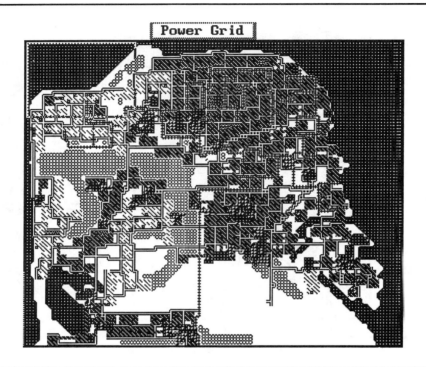

Figure 6-8.   The San Francisco Power Grid map after the earthquake

Another procedure can also represent the work of trained emergency crews in the hours immediately following a disaster, but this part of the scenario offers an extra gaming twist as well. In most scenarios, it is enough to have a power line running into a zone in order for that zone to be fully powered. In the San Francisco scenario, however, there are so many zones that have small damaged sections that you must watch out for power lines that connect to the damaged sections. If the power line connects to the damaged section, that zone is not powered. Keeping the power grid active is a major challenge in this scenario.

If you are efficient enough in these tasks, you will have some time left to rebuild the city. This will be tough, given your limited time and funds, but it is possible. As much as you can, try to rebuild in such a way that the transportation system becomes more efficient. Lombard Street, the "crookedest street in the world," may be a San Francisco tourist attraction, but there is no reason to keep it in your SimCity model. Use the earthquake as an opportunity to solve some of the transportation and land value problems covered in previous chapters. Then you will be sure to succeed.

Bomb Voyage: Hamburg

The same pre- and postdisaster emergency procedures that were discussed with regard to earthquakes are useful in winning the Hamburg, Germany scenario. This scenario features the challenge of disaster control after an Allied bombing raid during World War II (1944). Like the San Francisco scenario, this is a very difficult challenge, and your task is not only to halt destruction caused by the Allied bombing and to reconstruct the city, but to guide Hamburg to the Metropolis level and sustain that level to the end of five years in game time.

Before the bombing commences (and you only have a moment), you should construct a fire department. There are only two fire departments in Hamburg at the beginning of the scenario, which provides minimal protection, as shown in Figure 6-9. You can enhance the efficiency of your fire-fighting units considerably by placing one nearly anywhere on the map. If you can place one before the bombs begin to hit, you'll be ahead of the game.

Next, remember that the most important task at hand is to get the fires out. Figure 6-10 shows the widespread destruction and fires after the bombing that you will have to bring under control. Because you have limited fire-fighting forces at your disposal, you will want to make certain that you bulldoze around the fires as fast as possible. By creating these artificial firebreaks (a clear area of at least one square surrounding each edge of the fire tile), you ensure that the flames will eventually go out of their own accord. If you act fast during this early portion of the scenario, you will have significantly more time to rebuild and enhance the city before the end of the scenario. The challenge here, as in real life, is to react as quickly and efficiently as possible.

Once you've isolated the fires, meeting the victory conditions for the scenario is a relatively straightforward matter. Simply utilize some of

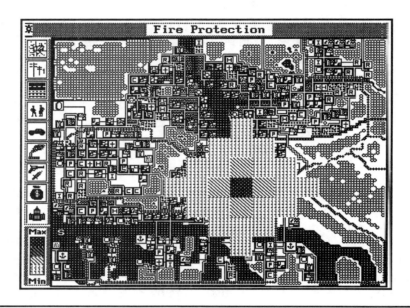

Figure 6-9.   The Hamburg Fire Protection radius map

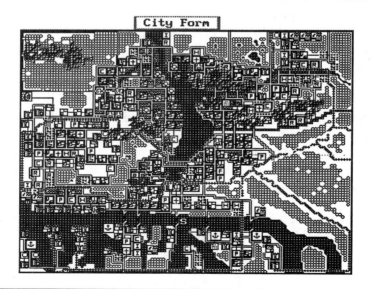

Figure 6-10.   The Hamburg City Form map after the bombing

the tips we've already covered on isolating the major problems via the map screen and correcting the highest priority problem each game year.

The Monster Is an Ecologist: Tokyo

The Tokyo, Japan (1957) scenario is a fanciful tribute to some of the "B-movies" of the late 1950s. During that era, teenagers squelched their fear of the atomic bomb with celluloid morality plays designed to assure them that the same science that had created the "monster" (which varied in the movies, but was probably symbolic of atomic destruction) could solve the problem it had created.

If you're ready to try your hand at being a "B-movie" mayor (and reversing the stereotype of ineffectiveness), you should load SimCity and select the Tokyo 1957 Monster Attack scenario. In this scenario, a giant gila monster (the folks at Maxis call him "Havana Gila") rises from the sea and heads directly toward the prime polluters in the industrial section of the city. In this case, the monster gives you, as the player, a chance to correct the damage wrought by technology in the city.

The goal of this moderately difficult scenario is to reach and maintain a city score of 500 or more within the five game years allotted. Of course, you have to accomplish all of this while undoing the damage wrought by Havana Gila. If you have done well at the scenarios treated earlier in this chapter, you should have no trouble with the Tokyo scenario. The secret of winning is essentially the same. You occasionally have time to add a fire department or two before the monster shows up. This increases your chance of getting the fires out more efficiently. Then you use the Bulldozer icon to isolate the fires.

This scenario is easier than the Hamburg and San Francisco scenarios because, instead of jumping from explosion to explosion, you have plenty of time to follow along behind the monster and bulldoze away until all the fires are isolated and the creature returns to the sea. If you also attempt to restore power wherever possible as you follow along behind the monster, you will maintain as much of your tax base as possible (by keeping the city functioning) and keep your score from falling too rapidly.

After you have completed that phase, winning is simply a matter of putting the pieces (zones, roads, rails, and so forth) back in a more efficient order than they were before.

Crash Course: Air Disasters

Perhaps the most ubiquitous disaster in SimCity is the airplane crash. Unless you are one of those relatively rare gamers who toggles all of the disasters off prior to playing SimCity so that you can build your city in peace, you have probably found that the pilots in SimCity crash quite frequently. Like airport planning commissions in the real world, you can attempt to foresee every possible difficulty, but the crashes are inevitable. You can place the simulated airport miles out of town and set the runways so that planes take off and land over water instead of over populated areas, but it doesn't stop the air disasters.

Fortunately, SimCity does not force you to deal with the loss of human life. You do not have to provide counseling for grieving families or adjudicate legal proceedings against allegedly negligent air traffic controllers. As in the other disasters discussed in this chapter, your responsibility is limited to containing the disaster's physical aftermath. If you have placed your airport away from populated areas, the best you can do is to be certain that your fire department containment radius is reasonably effective by placing fire departments where needed. Then use the Bulldozer icon to isolate the fire caused by the crash. Once the fire is out, you can rebuild without much difficulty.

Conclusion

Although you can simulate a multitude of disasters in SimCity, the methods of dealing with them are rather limited. Where structural and fire inspections, evacuation plans, fire access, and zoning limitations based on environmental impact reports are part of a city planner's arsenal of weapons against disasters, SimCity only allows you to mobilize for containment of damage to physical property. As a SimCity mayor, your options are few: zoning (not as useful in the game as in real life), ensuring adequate fire protection, and isolating disaster zones to ensure containment. Nevertheless, the brief introduction to emergency planning provided in this chapter and your gaming experiences should instill a new appreciation for what urban planners have to anticipate.

CHAPTER 7
THE BUCK STARTS HERE

This chapter is intended to serve as a "reality check." Using a case study of a fast developing area in Southern California (Temecula), the chapter will examine some problems that are not actually considered in the SimCity model, offer some tentative suggestions for dealing with those problems in the real world, and explain how you can build a scenario that will challenge you with some of the problems specific to the Temecula area.

Where on Earth Is Temecula?

There is a bumper sticker that offers a simple answer to this question: it reads "Where the Hell is Temecula?" in large print, and it answers the question in small print, "The Next Thing to Heaven." Early residents of this 90-square-mile valley must have agreed. The Native American name given to the region means "where the sun breaks through the mists." A more self-serving description was published in 1909. Entitled "The Historic Valley of Temecula: Thriving, Tempting Temecula of 1909," by Horace Parker, this early twentieth century "civic booster" pamphlet regaled its readers with such glowing prose as:

> ...the pearl of this paradise, the richest and fairest of all its tribe, is the fecundly, fertile, redundantly resourceful, surpassingly beautiful, and historic Temecula valley...

Temecula is located approximately 70 miles north of San Diego and 40 miles inland from the coastline near San Juan Capistrano (see Figure 7-1). This places the community within an hour's drive of metropolitan San Diego, Riverside, and Anaheim. In fact, Sea World and Disneyland are roughly equidistant from this "paradise."

The Wild, Mild West: Historical Summary

The Temecula Valley was originally settled by Native Americans. Archaeologists have uncovered evidence of more than 120 significant sites related to the hunting patterns of the Luiseno Indians, including thirteen probable village sites. The Luisenos, who built homes in semisubterranean lodges and worshiped (under the inspiring influence of datura, a narcotic drink derived from jimsonweed) an omnipotent, avenging god named Chungichnish, allegedly had no tribal name for themselves. Therefore, when the next influx of settlers, the missionaries of San Luis Rey de Francia, arrived in 1797, they called the Indians Luisenos, in deference to their conversion from the worship of Chungichnish to the Catholic faith.

By the middle of the nineteenth century, the Temecula Valley was valuable enough to fight over, as is proven by a bloody battle fought near the current site of Vail Lake Dam. After the Mexican-American War was resolved, the Temecula Valley was annexed to the United States.

As a stop on the Butterfield Overland Stage Route from St. Louis, Missouri to San Francisco, California, Temecula was known for a time (in the late 1850s) as the town where the outlaws "holed-up." Outlaw

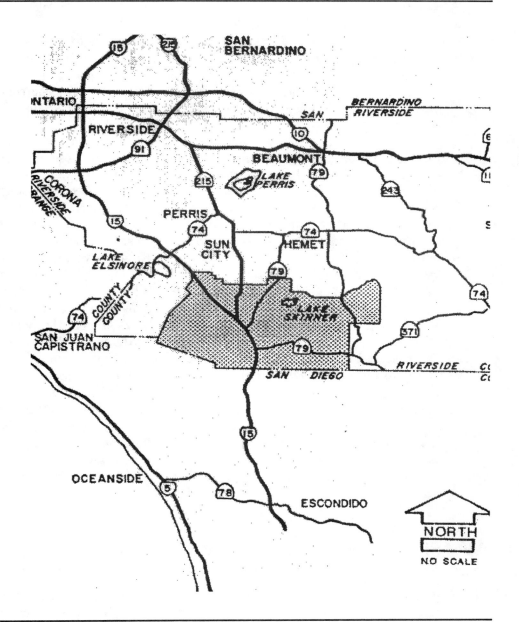

Figure 7-1.   Location of Temecula, California

gangs could "work" comfortably from San Diego to Los Angeles and return to the safety of Temecula's Front Street.

By 1882, as a result of the introduction of rail service to the historic western town, Temecula was booming. At the turn of the century, Temecula was known for three basic products: granite (quarrying began in the 1890s), cattle, and grain. Because it produced these basic commodities, Temecula became an important shipping point on the Santa Fe rail system.

In the twentieth century, Temecula continued its outlaw reputation. During the twenties and thirties, it served as a haven for those involved in organized crime, and for celebrities who were harried by their fans.

For SimCity players, the relevant portion of Temecula's history begins in the early 1960s. At that time, Kaiser Development Company, a subsidiary of the massive metal and chemical company, purchased the extensive holdings of the Vail Ranch (97,500 acres) for new residential, commercial, and light industrial development. Kaiser developed a master plan, which was reviewed and updated by the County of Riverside, subsequent to the purchase of Kaiser's interests by Bedford Properties, Inc. in 1986. Most of the information specific to the Temecula area that will be used in the remainder of this chapter is taken from the Southwest Area Community Plan Draft: Environmental Impact Report No. 217, prepared by the County of Riverside Planning Department.

In November of 1989, roughly a quarter of the area associated with the county study was incorporated into the new City of Temecula. A city council was elected in a general election, and a battle between perceived pro-growth and no-growth advocates on the council began, which continues to rage even now. A recall movement has been undertaken against two of the pro-growth council members, and turmoil seems likely. You will step into this power struggle when you play the "Simecula" scenario.

What SimCity Doesn't Tell You: Sensitive Areas

When I began to study the Temecula area, one major theme that kept recurring was that of protecting sensitive and irreplaceable resources (such as archaeological and paleontological sites, vegetation, and wildlife). To be sure, I had occasionally heard, in the past, of Greenpeace or the Sierra Club leading a crusade against development that endangers rare species of wildlife, but I rarely thought of them as existing in my own backyard. However, since I live in Temecula, this study brought these issues home to me in a very real way.

The Native American sites are everywhere. Heavy equipment operators must be extremely vigilant, because they never know when the next scoopful of earth might contain some invaluable physical artifact. In certain areas of the valley where previous finds have been relatively rich, the excavation crews must have resident archaeologists on site whenever earth is being moved. Figure 7-2 illustrates the known areas of archaeological sensitivity in the valley.

Paleontologists are also concerned about development in the Temecula area. As Figure 7-3 illustrates, Pliocene strata abound in the valley. Important fossils relating to primitive forms of antelopes, horses, mastodons, rabbits, and other mammals have been discovered in the course of residential and commercial development in the valley.

More than nine species of rare vegetation coexist in the Temecula Valley, and four rare species of wildlife may be found in or near the valley (Figure 7-4). These include the bald eagle (in the area surrounding Lake Skinner), Least Bell's vireo, the orange throated whiptail lizard (near the San Diego County line), and the Stephen's kangaroo rat (in the current development area).

The secret to managing development without losing these precious resources has been to excavate slowly, build preserves for wildlife and flora outside the development area, and halt development when necessary.

Reality Check   SimCity players who would like to add new elements of realism to their cities should simulate dealing with these potentially sensitive areas by disabling the Auto-Bulldoze function. Because Auto-Bulldoze enables you to excavate entire zones without even thinking about the individual parcels within the zone, it is obvious that potentially valuable resources are not being taken into consideration. Having to bulldoze each small plot simulates the idea that caring about sensitive environmental factors slows overall development. It has the added advantage of slowing the rate of your city's growth to a more realistic and desirable level. Those who play the "Simecula" scenario will be asked to play according to this restriction.

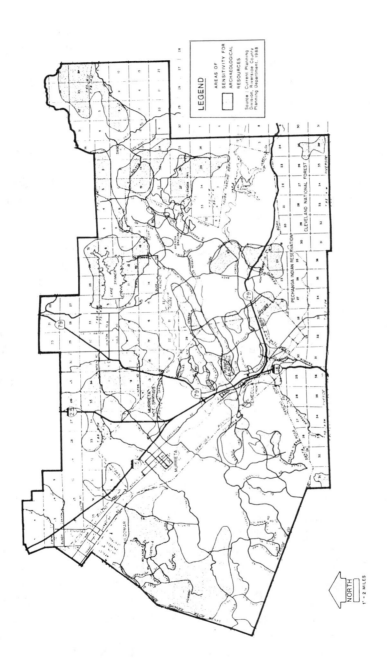

Figure 7-2. Archaeological sites in the Temecula Valley

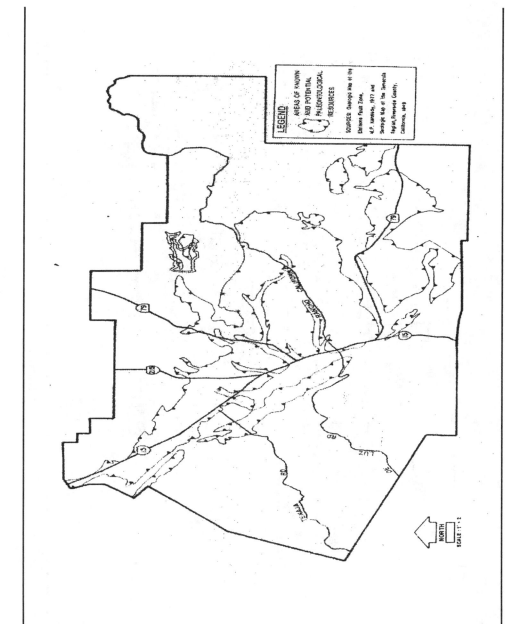

Figure 7-3. Sites of paleontological significance

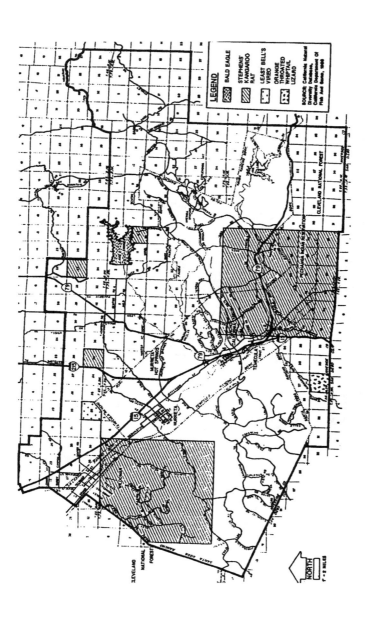

Figure 7-4. Endangered species of the Temecula Valley

What SimCity Doesn't Tell You: Services

This section will consider some of the standard formulae used by planners to determine and project needs for community services. Like the environmentally sensitive resources discussed earlier, many of these factors are not spelled out in the SimCity model, but suggestions will be made at the conclusion of this section for incorporating some limitations into your game play to reflect these problems.

Sims in White: Hospital Districts

In SimCity, hospitals appear in residential zones according to a relatively simple formula (see "Home Sweet Home: The Residential Zones Icon" in Chapter 1). In reality, the goal is to have a ratio ranging from 2.5 to 3 licensed beds per 1,000 people. In areas that are experiencing rapid population growth, the ratio is likely to become significantly out of proportion. Therefore, planning agencies have a responsibility to seek a balance between private and public health care providers.

In the Temecula area, full development is expected to reach a high of over three quarters of a million in population. The plan approved by the County of Riverside recognizes a need for 2,290 licensed beds. Because current facilities cannot provide that quantity of service, community leaders must be certain that there will be sufficient incentives for private facilities to expand, and that there will be funding for public facilities.

Another consideration that is important to hospital effectiveness, but is not dealt with in SimCity, is location. In Temecula, hospital facilities are not located near the primary industrial and commercial zones of the community. This is in keeping with the county planners' recommendation that hospitals, nursing homes, and schools be restricted from placement near pollution producing activities (Figure 7-5).

Reality Check   In order to simulate these considerations under the existing SimCity guidelines, you will need to consider two possibilities: land use restrictions and hospital bed-to-population ratio. In accordance with land use restrictions, you will want to bulldoze any hospitals that appear near the industrial or commercial center of the city. Then, you

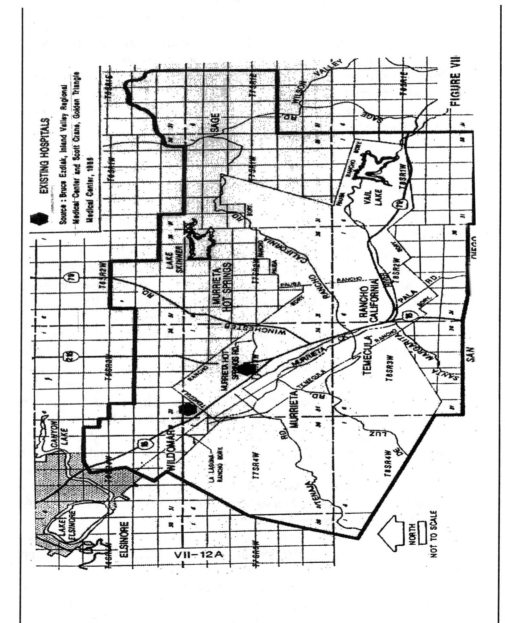

Figure 7-5.   Placement of hospitals in the Temecula Valley

should immediately zone some residential areas in the outlying areas of your community. At least one of them should appear as a hospital.

The second suggestion is harder to implement. It will require you to do some additional bookkeeping, but it offers an additional scenario for those who are willing to try something difficult. In simulating the hospital bed-to-population ratio, you are at a disadvantage because you cannot directly finance and build hospitals. However, you can monitor the population of your city via the annual report. Then assume each hospital on the board supports 250 licensed beds (this is generally high). Whenever the bed-to-population ratio falls below 3:1,000, you must zone enough residential zones to "construct" a hospital.

School Daze: School Districts

In SimCity, there is no representation of one of the most important problems faced by community leaders, constructing and staffing enough schools to adequately meet the needs of students. In general, school boards will utilize all the demographic information available to them, but projections for future growth will often be based on a student-per-dwelling unit (du) ratio. At the time of this writing, the local school district (servicing a population of less than 100,000) utilizes a ratio of .25 students per du. Using the same ratio, the school district expects to add one elementary school facility and expand from approximately 7,000 students at the time of this writing (four elementary schools, two middle schools, one high school, and one continuation school) to over 8,000 students in the next school year and over 15,000 students within five years.

Reality Check   As noted at the beginning of this discussion, there is no way to use the current SimCity program to model school district problems. Nevertheless, it is useful to perform a simple learning exercise with SimCity that may be illuminating to would-be urban planners. Figuring that 1,000 students would be a large student body for elementary schools and close to average for middle schools and high schools, you can pause the game and perform some simple calculations to determine how many school sites your city would probably need. Take the total population of your city from the evaluation screen and divide it by the 2.8 average persons per family, which is the highest persons-per-du rate used in the study. This will generate an approximate number of dwelling units for your city. Then multiply that number times .25 and you will get a projection of the total number of students you will need to provide for. Finally, divide the number of students by 1,000 to indicate the number of school sites you would need to provide for that many students.

If you find this interesting, you may also want to multiply the number of school sites times the equivalent funding for yearly police maintenance ($100). This artificial funding approach will tell you how much adding schools to your scenario would impact your city's budget. It should also demonstrate how conflicting needs draw from the same revenue sources (for example, the local property tax base). This is definitely not something you will want to do very often, but it is an eye-opening insight on the process.

Something Rotten in Temecula: Waste Management

Should the Temecula area (the city plus the immediately adjacent county areas) actually reach the full projected population of nearly three quarters of a million people, the environmental impact report estimates that an additional 47.4 million gallons of sewage per day would be added to the processing load of the treatment facility. In addition, the report estimates that the area would be inundated with approximately 572,211 tons of solid waste per day. As of the time of this writing, some consideration was being given to the possibility of creating new landfills in the open pits of played-out mines in the vicinity, but no final decision had, as yet, been made.

Reality Check   Since SimCity does not offer any icon or tile to represent waste management and treatment facilities, the dedicated SimCity player may wish to add to the challenge with a slight adaptation of the system. Sewage treatment facilities are not cheap. In terms of municipal budgets and expenditures, they would be (for our purposes) roughly equivalent to a traditional coal-powered power plant. Therefore, it would be feasible for you to place an extra (and unconnected) power plant on the map. What this would accomplish would be to simulate the drain of construction on your budget and visually suggest the need for a waste management facility. It would also add an additional air pollution producer to the mix. It should remain unconnected because it does not represent a power plant but rather a treatment plant.

Tiled Play: Parks and Recreation

Fortunately, SimCity does provide a Parks icon, and the opportunity to simulate actual planning for recreation and parks facilities. Unfortunately, it does not hold you to any kind of reasonable proportion between the actual population of the area and the number of acres dedicated to park facilities, nor does it offer an acreage-to-dwelling unit ratio. These are the primary units of measurement that urban planners use to determine the number of park facilities that are needed in a given community.

In Temecula, the master plan was originally established by the County of Riverside. The Riverside County planners delineated the average population per dwelling unit for each different type of residential density (2.98 persons for single family du with detached garage, or 2.72 persons-per-du for mobile homes). Then they projected a ratio of four acres of park facility for every 1,000 persons in the area's population. This projection suggests that the area will need an additional 1,163 acres of parks and recreation facilities in order to service the projected population of the area.

Unfortunately, the county's plans for funding the maintenance for the parks were rather haphazard. Originally, the county's funding plan scheduled individual subdivisions (that is, homeowners associations) to be assessed for park maintenance. In the spring of 1990, the City of Temecula created a citywide park district that included every parcel in the city.

Reality Check Because SimCity does not require maintenance funding for the park system, a major factor in the parks and recreation formula is missing. Although there is really no way to simulate the maintenance aspect of the parks and recreation formula, you can implement a relatively simple suggestion that will keep your city's park acreage in line with an established acreage-to-population ratio. Simply pause the game at the end of each game year. At that time, you can check your population on the evaluation screen and make a note of it. Assume that you are planting one acre for park use every time you utilize the SimCity Parks icon. Count the number of park tiles on your map. Make a note of the number and divide by four. If you have developed the right relationship between park land and population, you should be able to multiply the result times 1,000 and end up with the same number as your population. This activity will take some time, so be certain to pause the game during your calculations.

Kilowatt Kraving: Electrical Demand

While SimCity does force players to build power plants in order to service industrial, commercial, and residential demand, the program is fairly generous in its handling of the overall issues with regard to producing power. As noted in the section of Chapter 1 dealing with the power plants ("Power to the People: The Power Lines Icon"), SimCity does not currently offer enough energy choices, especially with regard to windmills, hydroelectric, and solar power, but the simulation does effectively indicate that producing power generates pollution.

The size of emissions (in pounds per day) from producing the power necessary to support a fully developed Temecula Valley are staggering, all the more so because they have been deemed "acceptable" in the Environmental Impact Report.

The potential problems of traditional power production are further exacerbated by the potential exhaust emissions from the increase in motor vehicles in a fully developed Temecula Valley. Under maximum development, motor vehicle emissions jump from 29,294 pounds of carbon monoxide per day to 372,368 pounds, and from 7,967 pounds of nitrogen oxides per day to 152,270 pounds.

Reality Check   SimCity is relatively accurate in terms of its handling of power generation. Take a look at Figure 7-6. This sketch indicates both projected and existing power substations. These projections are based on providing 6,081 kilowatt hours per dwelling unit per year, 36.6

kilowatt hours per square foot of office or retail space per year, and 10 kilowatt hours per square foot of manufacturing space per year. The pollution factor for coal plants in SimCity is also approximately commensurate with this projection.

To test out SimCity's handling of this issue, load the Hamburg, Germany city file. Note, however, that if you simply load the scenario and do not convert the city to a Saved City (.CTY) file, you will never have time to complete the experiment. To convert from a scenario to a Saved City (.CTY) file, simply load the scenario and save the city before doing anything else. Then you can return to the Main Menu screen and select the Load A City option. Select the file HAMBURG.CTY and you are ready for this experiment. Note the population and consider the number of power plants per 100,000 people. Then, compare this ratio to the existing number of substations noted in Figure 7-6. Note that the Temecula Valley currently has a population of less than 100,000.

The "Simecula" Scenario

In order to place you in the decision-maker's seat of a fast-growing, environmentally and archaeologically sensitive area like the Temecula Valley, try building your SimCity under the following constraints:

1. Using the zig-zag method, create a diagonal road moving from the upper northwest corner of the map screen to the lower southeast corner of the map screen. This represents Interstate 15.

2. Create two roads an equal distance apart running north and south. These represent the main feeder roads into Interstate 15, Winchester Road and Rancho California Road. (We are making them run north and south for the sake of convenience.)

3. Disable the Auto-Bulldoze feature to simulate a slowdown in development due to the existence of archaeological and paleontological areas of interest.

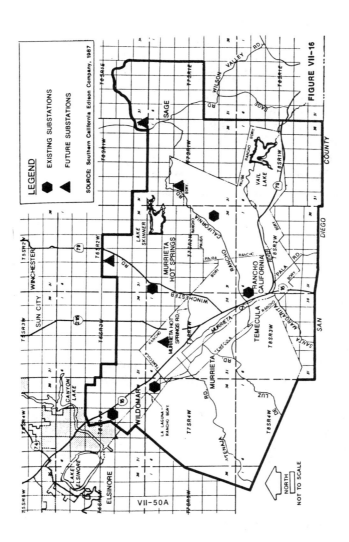

Figure 7-6. Existing and projected power substations

4. Place all industrial zones to the southwest of the diagonal road and most of the commercial zones immediately to the northeast of that road. This reflects the actual land use pattern in the city.

5. Limit the placement of hospitals to the north and west sectors of the map. This reflects both the recommended and actual land use pattern in the valley.

6. On the outskirts of the populated area, place an extra, unconnected power plant to symbolize waste management.

7. The object of the scenario is to reach a population of 500,000 with only moderate pollution before 40 game years have passed.

Conclusions

Will Wright once stated that his objective in creating SimCity was to get people to think about their own cities and the processes that were affecting them. By inspiring me to create the "Simecula" scenario, he has certainly succeeded in causing me to think about my community. Further, the guidelines suggested in this chapter, which go above and beyond the usual strategies for playing the game, should help you to create a new scenario using your own city or community.

CHAPTER 8
NURTURE IS NATURAL

If you have played the SimCity scenarios or have built one or more of your own cities prior to reading this chapter, you have probably noticed that every decision you make seems to affect aspects of the city that, in turn, affect other aspects of the city. At times, it seems as though every action creates a daisy chain of reactions that ripple through your city.

This is a valid assessment, because the program takes the view (as I do) that the world, regional areas, and each individual city function as portions of a larger organism. This larger organism is planet earth. This viewpoint is often referred to as the Gaia hypothesis, after the ancient goddess identified with the earth. This viewpoint recognizes that the conditions necessary for life are all interrelated in a sustained system of dynamic feedback.

Perhaps the simplest illustration of the hypothesis is the one given by James Gleick in *Chaos: Making a New Science*. He refers to a theoretical world with only three possibilities: white daisies, black daisies, and bare desert. In the analogy, he notes that the white daisies reflect light, making the temperature cooler. The black daisies like the cooler temperatures, so they proliferate over the bare ground and create a higher population of black daisies. In turn, the black daisies absorb light and make the planet warmer. Then, since the white daisies like the warmer temperatures, they proliferate and a cooler temperature is established, and the cycle continues. Of course, the environment eventually reaches an equilibrium. What happens when the factors sustaining that equilibrium are changed? Another equilibrium must be sought.

In a very real sense, every human endeavor upsets the equilibrium of this organism we call earth. The task of citizens, politicians, and planners in the real world is to carefully consider the direction in which we are "pushing the scales" when we upset the established equilibrium. In SimCity, your task is to conceive of a plan that integrates all the community's systems well enough that the organism functions smoothly on its own (and in relationship with hypothetical neighboring cities). This chapter will try to help you conceptualize some Gaia-influenced principles in order to build an organic city.

Entropy Is Not the Final Word

Adherents to the Gaia hypothesis point to the fact that entropy is relatively easy to measure in terms of heat and temperature, but they are not convinced of its validity when it comes to the formation of amino acids, microorganisms, and self-reproducing animals and human beings. In short, they believe that nature offers important clues to the possible states of equilibrium that planet earth can attain. Nature may be chaotic, but it is chaos with feedback.

Even so, there will be times in your SimCity experiences when you will feel like those "Sims" are running away with your city, and times when it seems like nothing you try can stem the tide of pollution, traffic, and low property values. You will be tempted to think that entropy has triumphed. Indeed, entropy is part of the SimCity design. If you do not learn to nurture your city, entropy will win. If you can learn how to nurture it, you can help your model city reach a new and beneficial equilibrium (at least, until the next crisis).

Case Study #1

You are playing a scenario in which you have designed a successful city and believe that you are moving triumphantly toward megalopolis. Then you discover that the land values are deteriorating in the central area of the city. Your choices are

a. Assume that this is part of the price of progress and simply continue playing as you were

b. Immediately bulldoze the zones with low land values and hope that your redevelopment will be successful

c. Attempt to discover the factors that are depressing land values and work on them

If you selected "a," you implicitly decided that entropy is inevitable and virtually wrote off as a lost cause the very area of the city that is potentially the most valuable. If you selected "b," you will discover a strange phenomenon. The new developments that appear will have the same problem. Redevelopment without solving problems does not work. Unrestrained crime will keep the prices down on the new developments, just as it will on the old ones. Traffic gridlock will still depress values in the new zones, because it will add to pollution, and pollution will depress property values.

The wise SimCity player will choose "c" and attempt to solve the problems in the areas with low land values rather than attempt redevelopment. There are several ways to determine where the problem lies. First, you can examine the City Dynamics chart that is included in the game. You will discover that crime and pollution are the factors that negatively affect land values. Then you can access the Crime map and Pollution map to ascertain whether the affected area suffers from either of those problems. Both problems usually contribute to low land values in the city center.

Now that you know that crime and/or pollution is affecting the area, you can move to the City Dynamics chart and look at the factors that influence crime or pollution. Because land value and police departments diminish the effects of crime, you may need to add an additional police department or two. Also, as noted in Chapter 3, you can build parks to increase the land values, which, in turn, provide a deterrent to crime.

Of course, if pollution is the major factor dragging down the property values, you will have some more difficult decisions to make. Pollution negatively affects land values, residential population, and the overall city score, but nothing specifically impacts pollution negatively. Therefore, you have to focus on industrial population, traffic, and radioactivity as the root causes of pollution.

If you have reached this point in the game, it is rather unlikely that you have adequate funds to construct a light rail system. Because the rail system carries an almost unlimited amount of traffic, this would reduce the pollution formula considerably. However, since you would very likely have to "float a bond issue" using the Fund option to accomplish this, many will want to avoid this alternative.

If you wish to reduce traffic without experiencing the high costs associated with public transportation, you must take the mountain to Mohammed. Because industrial zones are where many of your "Sims" are commuting to work, you may need to relocate both factories and housing. One of the handy quirks of SimCity is that it doesn't take long to rebuild an industrial zone after you bulldoze it. You can zone an area on the fringes of your map for a couple of relocated industrial zones and establish a couple of new residential zones within easy commuting distance. This, in turn, will leave you free to bulldoze a couple of inner city industrial zones and some of the problem residential zones. Then you can plant new parks and zone new residential areas.

This time, when you zone the residential areas, you should plant parks to limit the population density per residential zone. You can accomplish this by selecting the Bulldozer icon and clicking on one of the exterior plots of the residential zone. Then, before the program can build anything in the clear terrain you have just created, plant a park in that spot. This freezes the residential zone at the level of density it has attained at the time when the park is planted. By freezing the density at a lower level, you reduce a crime producing factor and indirectly help solve the land value problem.

Feedback Is Essential

Of course, one of the basic laws of physics is that for every action there is a reaction, and the dynamics of society are not an exception to this principle. The addition of industry in a new geographical location will impact another area with pollution and traffic.

For example, should you follow the suggestions outlined under Case Study #1, you will find that the new residences and the roads or rails established near the relocated industrial zones do not simply serve the close and convenient industries. Rather, you will find that the algorithms for traffic flow will cause traffic into the city center to increase as well.

This increased traffic flow will, in turn, create altered priorities for your simulated citizenry. So, it is important to utilize SimCity's feedback mechanisms in order to ensure that you are not creating insurmountable problems in some areas at the same time that you are trying to solve problems in others. For example, if your "Sims" are mostly concerned about traffic congestion, it isn't going to accomplish a lot to concentrate on altering the pollution map.

After you initiate each major project, you should allow the program to cycle past the end of the year. Then you should pull down the Evaluation window and note the top two concerns on the list. Next, you will want to access the Map window to determine the problem locations for the concerns that you have noted. This procedure will enable you to zero in on the problem areas and make the most efficient moves to improve the situation.

Another type of feedback in SimCity may be found in the messages that flash across the top of the screen like a Wall Street tickertape. When your citizens demand an airport or a stadium, it is a good indication that this is the right time to add such a factor into the equation. Yet each one of these public works projects brings its own set of problems with it.

Case Study #2

You are progressing quite nicely in developing Ghetto Junction, a city destined to be a metropolis. You have been keeping a cash reserve in the city's coffers, since you knew that eventually you would have to build a big ticket item like an airport. The time has come, but it brings up a multitude of new considerations.

First, where do you locate the airport? Some ideas were offered in Chapter 1 that may reduce potential grief. Second, how will it impact traffic? You should certainly expect that the addition of an airport will increase your overall traffic pattern. If your budget will allow it, consider linking the airport with your commuter rail network. This will soften the impact on inner city traffic somewhat. Third, how will it impact the economy of your city? It is true that adding an airport offers a multiplier effect to the internal economy. However, you will need more commercial zones in order to exploit that multiplier. Possible solutions include:

a. Bulldoze your downtown industries to make way for new commercial zones

b. Create a satellite commercial zone near the airport

c. Demolish residential zones to establish new commercial zones

d. Wait for the inevitable air crash and rebuild commercial zones wherever old zones are destroyed

The first choice would seem, at first glance, to be a viable one. After all, if your economy is shifting from one type of market factor to another, you would not need quite as many of the industries that contributed to the older market factor. Yet the industrial base is still important for several reasons. First, it affects population (without the industrial zones, the algorithm concludes that there are not enough jobs to support an equivalent population). It also affects the commercial viability of a city. There must be something to sell (manufactured goods), and the industrial zones impact directly on the commercial algorithm. Finally, the presence of industrial zones affects the overall city score (most major cities have some type of manufacturing base within their economy). Therefore, the smart SimCity mayor will not settle for simply replacing industrial zones with commercial zones.

Choice "c" is not viable because reducing residential population would immediately impact commercial success by reducing your potential market at the same time that you are expanding the competition. This means that you would receive no benefit from creating the commercial zones in the first place.

Choice "d" is a possible solution, but you should be very careful to keep a balance of industrial, commercial, and residential zones. If you replace the devastated areas with a surplus of commercial zones, it will not have a positive effect on your economy, because it will not have the appropriate industrial and residential modifiers to make the economy work.

In this case, choice "b" is the most viable. By creating commercial space near the airport, you are able to exploit the market multiplier without disrupting the established economic pattern in your central city. However, as the analogy of an organism warns us, watch out for sympathy pains in the rest of the city.

After you build an airport, you will have to be doubly certain that the fire protection radii overlap throughout the city. Once you have an airport, you will undoubtedly have air crashes, and you will need to stop those fires before they undo everything you've built up. Getting the fire protection levels up to par throughout the city will be an expensive proposition, not only in terms of new construction, but also in terms of the maintenance budget. Thus, you see once again how each decision impacts other areas of your city's budget.

Case Study #3

One SimCity mayor wrote to me with a unique plan for avoiding the political ramifications of pollution. It was suggested earlier in this book that you place the pollution producers on the outer extremities of your City map. He took an alternate tack. Recognizing that his citizens still complained about pollution, even when he took this advice, he decided to place all his pollution producers on a large island in the center of his map. If he did not immediately get the right terrain to accomplish this, he rejected the random terrain until he got what he was looking for.

Next, he built a rail system connecting the industries on the island to each other and to the mainland. Thus, he was not adding automobile emissions as a source of pollution. Then he planted parks on every available plot of shoreline located on both mainlands opposite the industrial island. This, he reasoned, would provide a buffer zone against air pollution (the algorithm doesn't recognize this, but it makes logical sense outside of the game's context).

Having accomplished this major task, he proceeded to zone residential and commercial zones all over the mainland according to his usual pattern. He even managed to use regular roads on the mainland in order to avoid the high maintenance costs associated with the rail system.

As a result, he noted that he still had plenty of pollution, but he rarely had more than 8 percent of the "Sims" complain about the pollution. Of course, you can imagine some of the other problems he encountered. The organic analogy holds in his example as well. Because the residential zones were located far away from the city center, property values started out at a relatively low level. The parks on the shoreline helped, but having all the residential areas together with low property values contributed to crime, which caused a further spiral downward in property values.

Hence, his "Sims" were continually complaining about the crime rate and he had to build extra police stations to both fight crime and, indirectly, increase the land value. Building the police stations turned out to be expensive both in terms of construction and funding.

Conclusion

This chapter explored some of the significance of the Gaia hypothesis for SimCity players. By examining the case studies, you should have discovered that the SimCity algorithms treat the cities you construct as organisms. The observations noted in the case studies will help you understand the consequences of the major planning decisions you will make in SimCity and enable you to avoid some potential problems.

If you have learned the lessons in this chapter, you will have observed that nurture is the antithesis of entropy, attention to feedback enables you to focus on potential solutions, and every action provokes a string of reactions. How you juggle those three realities will determine how successful you will be in playing SimCity.

CHAPTER 9
ARCHIVES OF THE PLANNING COMMISSION

One of the fastest ways to master a skill is to observe how others perform the same task. This chapter will allow you to do just that, as it unveils some classic mistakes and coups accomplished by other players. Some of the material may repeat hints given in other sections of the book, but the use of specific illustrations should help you visualize potential mistakes and miscues.

What's Wrong with This City?

In Figure 9-1, you will notice an early attempt by this author to design a city. The basic error should be obvious, and it is replicated at several different locations. Have you guessed? The problem concerns the roads. Note that almost all of the roads dead-end into their target zones. This

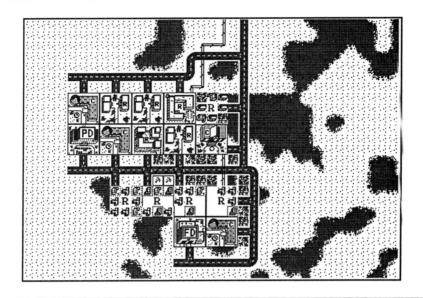

Figure 9-1.   What's wrong with this city?

means, among other things, that there is no real thoroughfare to handle the continuity of traffic flow within the city. Thus, instead of traffic flow, you end up with numerous traffic bottlenecks.

This error caused another problem as well. You never have enough land to build on, and the way these roads were designed, you have even less usable land than usual. All of those extra angles have created small plots of land, many of them too small even to plant as park space.

In actuality, the error was a consequence of not reading the documentation. I assumed that a road had to "end" in a zone in order for the road to service that zone. This is not true, because any road that touches one side of a zone provides ingress to the zone.

The Airport Blues

As if my *faux pas* with road ingress and egress wasn't bad enough, the airport fiasco (see Figure 9-2) was the *coup de grace*. Following hints

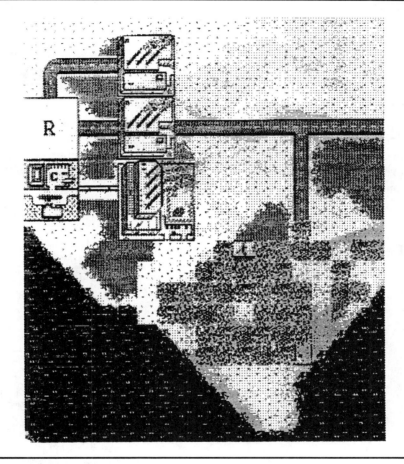

Figure 9-2. **The airport blues**

from the publisher of SimCity, I tried to place the airport next to water and away from the center of the city. Yours truly also thought it would be really clever to isolate some of the city's industry in the area near the airport. Can you spot the airport? Actually, the only remaining portion of the airport is the tile with the animated radar dish on it. It is still animated, interestingly enough, even though the airport was devastated in the aftermath of an air disaster.

How did this devastation occur? The simple truth is that the genius who concocted this airport, complete with its own industrial park, neglected to construct a fire department anywhere near the airport and environs. Therefore, when a plane crashed at the end of the runway and a fire began, there was no fire protection sufficient to stop the fire. So the airport burned to the ground and left the city $10,000 poorer, but with a much wiser mayor.

What can you learn from this experience? Be certain to check your fire protection capability on a regular basis. This is particularly appropriate when you begin to spend larger sums of money on capital improvements. If you lose an airport, seaport, or stadium, it will take a long time for you to make up lost ground.

Derailing Mass Transit

Mass transit is a wonderful addition to any SimCity. However, the mayor of the city depicted in Figure 9-3 has made a typical mistake. Is it

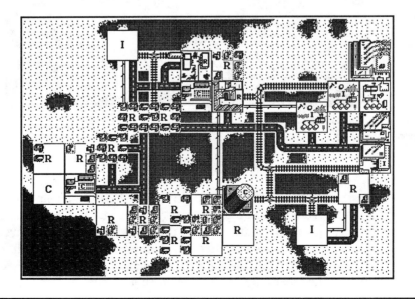

Figure 9-3. Derailing mass transit

obvious to you? Just as the mayor in Figure 9-1 failed to provide for traffic continuity with his road grid, the mayor in Figure 9-3 has created several rail lines that do not connect to any central line. In this configuration, it would be impossible to travel from the east side of the map to the west side of the map via rail. Further, the use of so many right angles created unusable plots of land, just like the ones that resulted from the poor road grid in Figure 9-1.

What's Right About This City?

On the brighter side, the city depicted in Figure 9-4 is rather well thought out. The industrial zones are clustered together on the outskirts

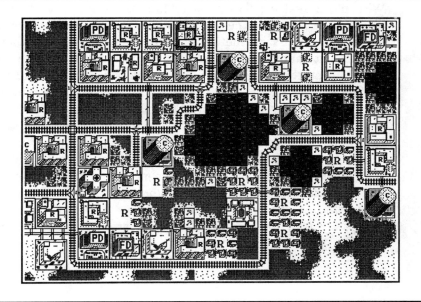

Figure 9-4. What's right about this city?

of the city (not pictured); the commercial zones are located in clusters with plenty of open park space around them; and virtually the entire city is serviced by an interconnecting rail line. In addition, the planner has ensured that the residential zones will retain their value by placing a large percentage of them around bodies of water and by building police departments at regular intervals.

Note that both commercial strips in this city have at least three zones that have attained the highest commercial density (symbolized by round towers). Compare this with the commercial strips in Figure 9-5 and you will readily perceive that to place too many commercial zones together without including several residential zones in the vicinity is not wise. Of course, reaching the maximum commercial density is valuable to your overall tax base, so you will want to strive to produce these skyscrapers whenever possible. To balance the extra high commercial density, however, the planner has chosen to surround the towers with open space. This is a strategy that Le Corbusier would have approved, and it should be emulated by modern planners, as well.

It is interesting to note that in this design the fire departments are spaced more widely than the police departments. This is quite logical, because it is easier to put out occasional fires than it is to fight crime. Without the extra police departments, the crime rate would rise and devalue the land, but the fire protection radius does not directly affect land value (unless, of course, there happens to be a fire that your fire department cannot put out). Therefore, it is more possible to fudge on the fire protection radius that it is on the police protection radius.

You may also notice that the planner has utilized a useful transportation trick for this community. The most urban section of the city is replete with mass transit, but many of the suburban areas are serviced by traditional roads (not shown here). In many ways, this is like the Victor Gruen strategy (discussed in Chapter 5), which attempted to isolate vehicle traffic outside of the central city of Fort Worth. In both this city and the design for Fort Worth devised by Gruen, traditional roads stop on the outskirts of town. This is sometimes called an *intercept strategy* for creating downtown areas conducive to pedestrian traffic.

Never Tampa with Tampa Bay

In Figure 9-5, you can observe a portion of a detailed SimCity map of Tampa Bay, Florida, designed by Richard K. Brown of the county tax assessor's office for Hillborough County, Florida. In order to create the right scale in depicting Tampa Bay as it actually exists, Mr. Brown had to ignore certain features of the SimCity model. He indicated that he was fully aware that his decisions were not conducive to creating a more efficient SimCity, but he wanted to play with the land in Tampa Bay as it was actually being utilized. This is relevant to you, because his intentional decisions illustrate two very common mistakes that are often accidentally committed by SimCity players.

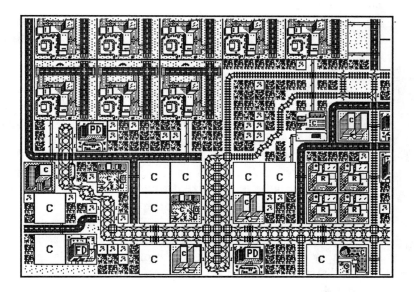

Figure 9-5. Tampa Bay, Florida

First, Mr. Brown noted that the airport terrain tile that the program uses was not sufficiently large to reflect the actual land required for a metropolitan airport. To reflect this actual space requirement, he zoned twenty airports (eight pictured) on his map. Many novice SimCity players are tempted to construct multiple airports in order to enhance the commercial value of their cities. This does not work. One airport, two airports, or twenty airports all have the same effect on a city. The SimCity program simply checks to see if an airport is in operation or not. The same principle holds for seaports, because there is no extra multiplier for multiple seaports either.

One penalty for having extra airports is the fact that airports are pollution producers. Adding extra airports for aesthetic or cartographic purposes also adds a considerable amount of extra pollution into the city's atmosphere. Unless you are determined to render an accurate proportional representation of an existing airport, multiple airports are not a good idea.

The good news is that there can be only one plane in the air at a time, regardless of the number of airports. So at least those who choose to add extra airports in modeling real cities will not be penalized with extra air crashes.

Another aesthetic factor has to do with all of the rail loops. Although this is extremely realistic for purposes of modeling Tampa Bay, there is a tremendous penalty in terms of SimCity's scoring system. Each one of those curves is an inefficient stretch of track that must be maintained at the same cost as the useful sections of track. All of those curves and double-trackage act as leeches on the city transportation budget.

Another aesthetic decision that caused Mr. Brown to be penalized by SimCity may be observed in the open space immediately to the south and to the southeast of the airport. In SimCity these park areas enhance the land value of surrounding zones, but they do not add to the tax base. In actuality, the park area due south of the airport is the training camp for the Tampa Bay Buccaneers professional football team. As such, you would expect that the land would be taxed (although some cities are rather too lenient with their sports teams). The park area to the southeast of the airport represents a commercial bonanza for which the player receives no profit in SimCity. This is the Hall of Fame Inn, Golf, and Racquet Club. It is unfortunate that the program does not allow you to make your own tax assessment on individual pieces of property as the game progresses.

The realistic portrayal of Tampa Bay worked against the game's scoring system in another way. Note how many different commercial zones are stacked together in one general area. This is not the commercial strip idea found in Figure 9-4. In the master-planned community of Figure 9-4, the commercial strips were not only surrounded by open spaces, but were also in close proximity to residential zones. In the Tampa Bay section displayed on the map, there are not enough residential zones in the vicinity to support the number of commercial zones in use. Thus, you do not see those zones as well developed as in the positive model.

Final Evaluation

As this chapter should illustrate, mastering SimCity is a process and not something that is accomplished overnight. The experience of playing SimCity should open your eyes to the difficult choices inherent in actual city planning, provide stimulus and entertainment as you attempt to solve the problems of an urban area evolving toward megalopolis, and create an interest in the fast-moving political world around you. The illustrations (sometimes confessions) presented in this chapter should offer enough negative and positive examples to allow you to improve your performance as a SimCity mayor and to avoid some of the mistakes made by others. SimCity is a rewarding experience that should contribute to your understanding of the world around you.

APPENDIX A
USING THE TERRAIN EDITOR

For some players, simply designing a city with the editing tools provided in the SimCity program is not enough. Many of these players want to re-create a particular city or design their own terrain maps to work from. Other players want to build channels connecting their waterways in order to avoid repetitive and costly shipwrecks. Finally, some players will want to modify their saved cities so that they can increase population and reach the tantalizing goal of megalopolis. To meet the needs of these players, Maxis Software offers a *Terrain Editor*.

The Terrain Editor is included with the Macintosh and DOS versions of SimCity Classic, and a free offer for the Terrain Editor is included in SimCity Classic for Windows. It is also available for the Amiga. Interestingly enough, it is built into the C-64/128 version. The Macintosh and Amiga versions do not work exactly the same way as the IBM (the menus are slightly different), but the functions are the same in all three versions. On the IBM, it can be installed to a hard disk or run from a floppy disk.

Note: IBM users should be aware that the Terrain Editor is packaged with either 5.25-inch or 3.5-inch disks (not both). Make sure that you purchase the format that you need.

The purpose of this appendix is to provide basic instructions for using the Terrain Editor and to describe briefly the city files that come standard on the Terrain Editor disk.

Let There Be Light: Installing the Disks

On the IBM PC and compatibles, there is an Install program provided on Disk 1. If you have a hard disk, simply place Disk 1 into your A drive and type **INSTALL**. The program will prompt you to answer a series of questions, and it will double-check each step of the process with a "N/Y" prompt. If everything is all right, simply press ENTER and the process will continue. If something is wrong, type **N** and then press the ENTER key. The program will allow you to correct the error. When all the questions are answered and you are given a final chance to double-check the information provided, the program will copy all of the pertinent files on Disk 1 into your SimCity directory on the hard disk. Then you will be prompted to insert Disk 2, so that the pertinent files from that disk may be copied. Note, however, that the prefabricated cities provided on Disk 2 are not automatically copied to the hard disk. If you wish to have them on your hard disk, you will need to use a DOS command. Insert each disk and type:

COPY A:*.CTY C:\SIMCITY

All of the predesigned cities will be copied to your hard disk.

If you are installing the program on separate floppy disks, you will need to format either two low-density disks or one high-density disk to hold both the program and the prefabricated city files. Then insert Disk 1 and type **INSTALL**, just as you would in the hard disk procedure. Instead of answering that you are installing to your C disk, however, you should answer that you are installing to the B disk (or A disk if you only have one floppy drive). Note that the Install program does not automatically copy the predesigned city files to your new disk. Insert each disk and type,

COPY A:*.CTY B:\

which will copy the files to your new disk(s).

With the Amiga and Macintosh versions of the Terrain Editor, there is no Install program. You simply copy the Terrain Editor files to the SimCity directory on your hard disk. Then you double-click on the Terrain Editor icon, and you are ready to design your landscape. If you are installing to a floppy disk, you simply copy the Terrain Editor files to a formatted floppy disk. Then you can boot from your usual boot disk, select the Terrain Editor icon from your new disk, and get set to design your world.

If you are using the Terrain Editor from a floppy disk, insert the disk in your A drive and type **TERRAIN**. If you are using the Terrain Editor from your hard disk, change to the SimCity directory (usually by typing **CD\SIMCITY** at the C> prompt) and type **TERRAIN**. Either procedure will call up the program, providing an Edit Window that looks very similar to the SimCity screen. The major difference between the Edit Window and the SimCity screen is that there is no terrain on this map as yet.

At this point, you have two basic choices. You can use the modified random terrain generator or you can construct a new world, one terrain tile at a time. The modified random terrain generator, like the random terrain generator in the basic SimCity program, is a quick method of creating terrain. The advantage of using the modified version that comes with the Terrain Editor software is that you can designate the number of trees and lakes, choose the degree of crookedness in the rivers, and decide whether there will be islands or not. The Amiga version has a special feature that none of the others has—it allows you to overlay a grid on the map window. Typing **G** toggles this grid on and off. This can be extremely useful whenever you want to copy the land features of a real city from a map. Just draw a similar grid on the map and enter the terrain in small sections at a time.

In the tile-by-tile mode, you use the cursor to designate each square of forest, lake, or river. Then, after you have placed the terrain features in the appropriate places, you can order the computer to smooth the straight edges and give the map a lifelike appearance.

Fortunately, the Terrain Editor is so versatile that you are not restricted to one method or the other. If you so choose, you can begin with the modified random terrain generator in order to establish the basic terrain. Then you can use the tile-by-tile approach to put the finishing touches on your new map. Another option is to load an existing city into the Terrain Editor and use the tile-by-tile approach to fine-tune that city for further development.

Let the Land Be Separate from the Waters: Menus

Those familiar with the SimCity commands will have no trouble with the Terrain Editor. There are three different pull-down menus that operate the editor. They may be accessed via the mouse, by keyboard control of the cursor, or by typing the keyboard codes. You can access the System menu by pressing the ALT key and typing S. This menu enables you to print a city in a reduced format on one page or as a multipage poster, just like the same command in SimCity. It also permits you to start a new city (without the Terrain Creation Parameters, like the random terrain generator built into SimCity) or load a city (this option also lets you load in saved terrain). Finally, the System menu includes options for saving a city (under a new name or under an old name) and for exiting the program.

The second pull-down menu, the Terrain menu, accessed by pressing the ALT key and typing **T**, is where most of the Terrain Editor work takes place. Using the Clear Map command (via the cursor or by pressing the CTRL key and typing C) enables you to remove everything and start all over. You don't even have to worry about a messy flood a la Genesis. If, on the other hand, you like the terrain itself, but don't care for what humanity has done to it, you can use the Clear Unnatural Objects command to remove all evidence of the handiwork of mankind. You can wipe a city off the face of your SimEarth by simply loading it into the Terrain Editor and using the Clear Unnatural Objects command. The program will wipe out everything except the natural terrain features, using a broadcast-style dissolve from left to right.

From the same menu you can also access the modified random terrain generator. Click the mouse button on the command Generate Random Terrain or press the CTRL key and type **T**. This will bring up a window with three different sets of numbers on it. The numbers represent the amount of trees and lakes, and the degree of crookedness (the program calls it curviness) of the rivers. By clicking the mouse button on the up and down arrow buttons, you determine the percentage of land covered by trees and lakes, and you set the number of curves (which must be greater than one) in any rivers. Another important option under this pull-down menu is the *smoothing function*. This function allows you to smooth only the trees and rivers or simply to smooth everything. Without this function, your map will look like a pattern of squares and rectangles, which would not be very convincing. Also, you will probably want to use the smoothing function after removing unnatural objects in order to improve the appearance of the terrain. Note the terrain with buildings in Figure A-1. Figure A-2 shows the same terrain with all unnatural objects removed, using the Terrain Editor. Notice how much more natural the terrain looks after smoothing it (Figure A-3).

Another important function within this menu is the *island function*. Whenever you use the island function, the very next map to be generated will always be an island.

Figure A-1.   Terrain with buildings

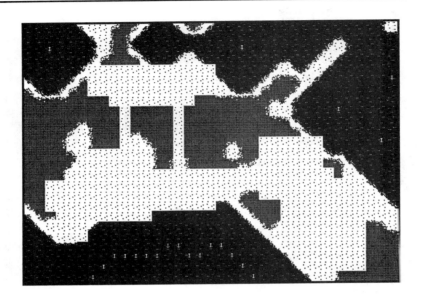

Figure A-2.   Terrain after unnatural objects are removed

The third pull-down menu allows you to adjust some of the game's parameters. Clicking the mouse button on Name & Level allows you to change the name of a city and adjust the game play level at which you saved the city. For example, you many have saved a scenario at the Easy level and, as a consequence, discovered that you were going to win too easily. Using this function, you could reset the game to Medium and come back to it with expectations of a greater challenge.

Also, if there is one thing gamers like, it is the ability to cheat with impunity. Selecting the Game Year option allows you to do just that. You can reset the pointer that handles the date in order to go back in time and fix some of the problems your city may be facing. You can also reset the date, save the game, and astound your friends by showing them how far you've gotten (at least, how far you want them to think you've gotten) in such a short amount of time. You can also toggle the sound on and off from this menu.

Figure A-3.   Smoothed terrain

The Tile Waits on No Land

The editing tools in the Terrain Editor are even simpler than those in SimCity itself. The icons are labeled: Dirt, Trees, River, Channel, Fill, and Undo. The first three represent obvious terrain types (clear, forest, and water). The other three represent important functions. The Channel icon lets you establish the permissible route for ships to travel. This feature allows you to avoid a lot of grief by minimizing the potential for shipwrecks. Note, however, that ships must have a functioning seaport and that the boat channel must lead to the edge of the map in order for the ship traffic to work properly. Ships cannot appear in landlocked lakes, for example.

The Fill icon functions just like a Fill command in a paint program. When you click on this icon, the active area fills with trees, water, channel, or dirt (depending on which of the first four icons you last selected). Macintosh owners should note that the Fill function is not available from a menu in the Macintosh version. Instead, you simply type **F** and the area will fill. Finally, the Undo command allows you to perform damage control whenever you have made a mistake. Clicking on Undo rescinds your last action.

C-64/128 owners should note that there is no simple way to turn water into land. However, if they build bridges over the sections of water which they want to turn into land and, believe it or not, burn the bridges, the rubble will become land.

A Tale of Nine Cities

Along with the editing tools, the Terrain Editor provides you with nine new challenges. There are nine cities with nine distinctive personalities and at least nine different problems. This section of the appendix will summarize the various cities in order to help you prepare to solve these problems.

Bad News City

Bad News City offers an extremely challenging situation for the advanced SimCity player. Explosions shatter the mayor's peace of mind every few minutes; fires flare wildly through vast sections of the city (Figure A-4); and major sections of the metropolis are out of power. You will need to bulldoze large sections of the city and rapidly build a couple of power plants in order to get things partially under control. That's the good news! The bad news is that the explosions just keep on coming.

Big City

Big City has more than its share of problems. Fortunately, however, it doesn't have explosions every few minutes. To be sure, this city has a high crime rate, but the readers of this book know how to plant parks and build new precincts. The city has also had a meltdown in the past.

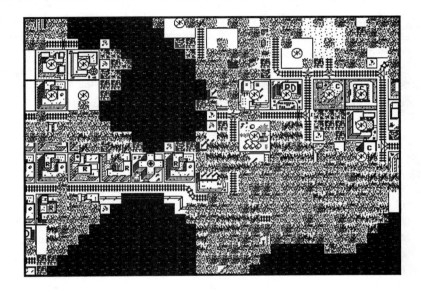

Figure A-4. *Fires after an explosion in Bad News City*

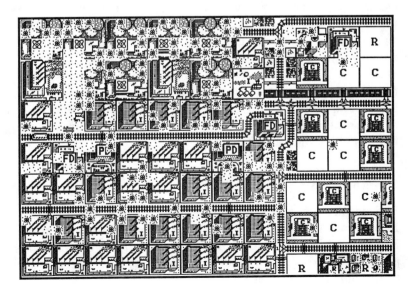

Figure A-5. *An irradiated area in Big City*

There is still evidence of a radiation spill (Figure A-5), and you'll have to work around that. You may want to bulldoze around it so that you can reconnect the rail system. You might even want to build some new coal-driven power plants on the outskirts of the city to take some of the burden off those nuclear power plants. In addition, you should note that there are plenty of commercial and residential zones that are not being occupied. Try to find a way to attract some occupants.

Deadwood City

Deadwood City is aptly named. The city not only begins at an early enough level that it has a low population, but the initial city design is full of duplication (that is, deadwood). First of all, there is no reason to have so many different stadiums in the center of the city (Figure A-5). Only one is needed to satisfy the demands of the citizenry. The others are not only expensive, but wasteful. Second, there are all sorts of traffic circles throughout the traffic grid that really serve no purpose whatsoever (Figure A-7). They not only create potential for traffic jams, but they add additional maintenance costs to the city's road budget.

Third, the separation of each of the three major types of zones from each other (having the residential zones so far from the industrial and commercial zones, and so on, as shown in Figure A-8) causes two problems. First, it guarantees a long commute for those who live in the residential areas. Second, it keeps land values lower than they should be, because the city has no authentic economic center. If you load Deadwood City and call up the Land Value map from the Map Window menu, you will note that the land value is uniformly low over the entire map. Compare that with Tokyo's map, for example, and note the difference. You do need an economic center to your city in order to keep the tax base high and the citizenry happy.

Finigan City

Believe it or not, this is a completely empty city, as shown in Figure A-9. If you want to take a gigantic island, complete with peninsula, and turn it into a metropolitan paradise, this is your opportunity. Just like the pioneers of old, you have the opportunity to go from zero population up to the hundreds of thousands.

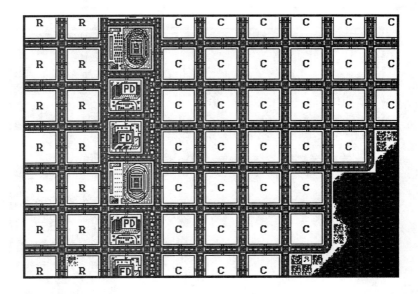

Figure A-6.   The stadiums of Deadwood City

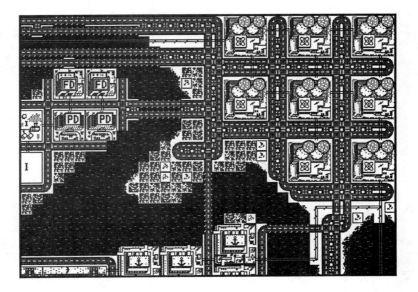

Figure A-7.   Traffic circles in Deadwood City

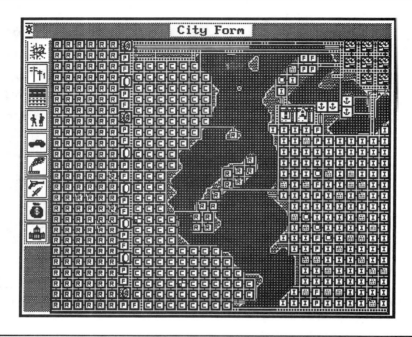

Figure A-8. The City Form map of Deadwood City

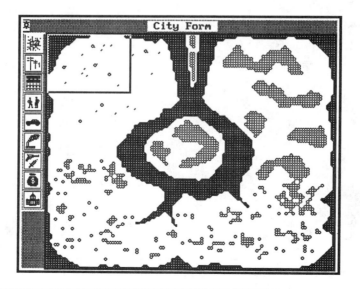

Figure A-9. The City Form map of Finigan City

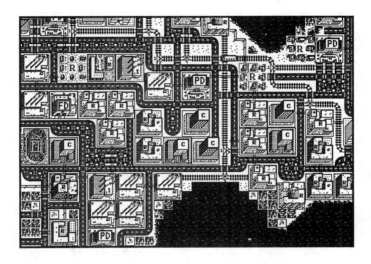

Figure A-10. A traffic snarl in Fredsville

Fredsville

Those of you who thought the Bern, Switzerland scenario was too easy should take a look at Fredsville. Fredsville has a limited rail network and massive traffic jams (Figure A-10). Your mission, should you decide to accept it, is to straighten out the traffic snarls and build enough new roads and rails to establish a respectable, comfortable city.

Happy, IL

It isn't clear whether this city is based on a real midwestern city or not. What is clear, however, is that this city of happiness has a high approval rating for the mayor, pollution isolated into one industrial section (Figure A-11), and a vast amount of parkland to keep the citizenry content (Figure A-12). As the city evolves, you will face the same basic problems you would find in any city, but this city gives you the best base to work from of any city on the Terrain Editor disk.

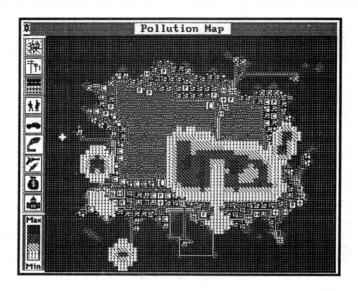

Figure A-11.   The Pollution map of Happy, IL

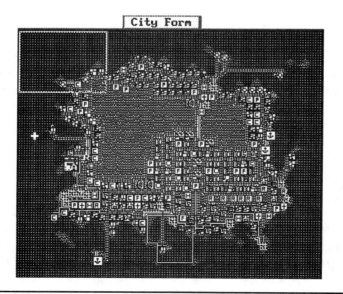

Figure A-12.   The City Form map of Happy, IL

Figure A-13. The Crime map of Joffeberg

Joffeberg

The challenge for the player who loads this city is to get the crime rate down. You will barely have time to answer the protection quiz before you receive word that crime is running rampant throughout the city (Figure A-13). Note the lack of adequate police protection and try to build more parks in order to reduce the crime rate.

Linear City

This city reminds me of some of the small cities I used to encounter along U.S. Route 66. These cities were often completely dependent upon business generated by tourism, so they tended to line up all along the major highway (Figure A-14). Notice that Linear City also has a tre-

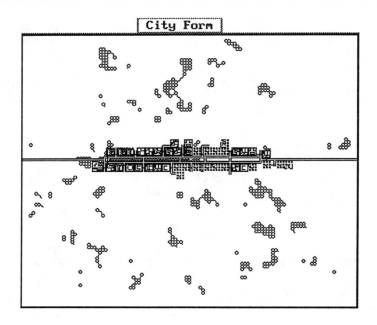

Figure A-14.   The City Form map of Linear City

mendous pollution problem all along its western edge. This problem can be mitigated with new parks and further development away from the industrial center.

Medieval City

Medieval City is an island city reminiscent of a medieval fortress built around a seaport (Figure A-15). There is plenty of room to expand throughout the rest of the island, and its growth reflects the historical process of a city expanding from a seaport economy to a more balanced and diverse economy (see Chapter 2 for a discussion of this phenomenon).

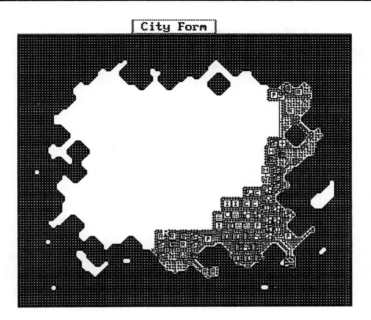

Figure A-15. The City Form map of Medieval City

And It Was Good

The Terrain Editor makes a great simulation even better. By allowing you to edit the terrain, it enables you to follow authentic geographic patterns or to let your imagination roam free. The library of cities (nine on the IBM, and more on the Amiga and Macintosh) is creative, and it offers you brand new challenges.

APPENDIX B
A SIMCITY ATLAS

Once you've begun to master some of the intricacies of the SimCity program, you will have a natural curiosity about how your work compares with that of other SimMayors. This appendix offers a brief description and annotation of several cities that were entered in SimCity competitions. As you've seen in earlier chapters, it is possible to learn both from the successes and from the failures of others. Screen shots depicting the situations and techniques described in the text are shown at the conclusion of this appendix.

Geometric Cities

Many cities are designed with particular geometric principles in mind. The designers are concerned about balance, symmetry, and shape (sometimes to the point of losing sight of function). This section will examine three cities that take these principles to an extreme: Quadripoli, Squaresville, and Symmetry.

Quadripoli

The SimMayor of Quadripoli is a witty fellow named Joe Roosth. Joe calls this city a "metropolis for the simple-minded." His rationale for criticizing his city is its lackluster master plan, which calls for every block to be roughly equivalent in size and composed of four zones each, positioned in either a square or rectangular format (see Figure B-1). Joe notes that the major problem in the city is pollution, yet his construction of a city that relies entirely upon a light rail system to provide its transportation grid and his use of a nuclear power plant to fuel the power grid ensures that the highest concentration of pollution is located in the heavy industrial areas (unless, of course, there is a nuclear disaster). The maximum levels of pollution (Figure B-2) could have been lessened if the mayor had not chosen to concentrate all of the heavy industry into a single area (Figure B-3).

Examine Figure B-1 again. Even a novice SimCity player is likely to notice that there is considerable unused and seemingly purposeless open space between the blocks. Indeed, there are even several inefficient rail approaches to many of the zones, of the type discussed in Chapter 9. How then, you may well ask, did Mr. Roosth manage to get such an efficient economy (Quadripoli runs great on a seven to nine percent tax rate) and such a high population with so much inefficiency? Here, again, is the magic of the Terrain Editor. In the basic SimCity game, there is a minimum percentage of hydrographic terrain (water coverage) on every random map. With the Terrain Editor, you can edit the terrain to create bodies of water shaped exactly like you want them, and you can place the exact amount of hydrographic terrain you wish. Without the Terrain Editor, you must maximize every bit of land that is available to reach this point of efficiency.

Squaresville

Walter Hill submitted the Squaresville plan to the SimCity design contest, sponsored by Maxis Software. It is immediately obvious that Mr. Hill used the Terrain Editor, without using the smoothing function described in Appendix A, in order to create the square central city bordered by a man-made waterway and greenbelt (Figure B-4).

The design of Squaresville offers some distinct positives. First, the proximity of water and the greenbelt ensures that the property values in the central city get near-maximum modifiers. Since the SimCity program calculates those as positive factors, along with the geographical center of the city (see "For the People: Managing Land Value" in Chapter 3), Squaresville has a very valuable central city (Figure B-5). Second, the placement of somewhat concentrated industrial areas separated by water and forest, along with the almost exclusive use of rail transportation, means that pollution is held to acceptable levels (see

Figure B-6). It is still the number one concern of the "Sims" in Squaresville, but it is low enough that the SimMayor has a marvelous approval rating (over 80 percent during the experimental play for the writing of this appendix).

Symmetry City

Designed by Jon Dodd of Braintree, Massachusetts, Symmetry City won the second prize in the Maxis Software contest. This city is so symmetrical in terms of function, as well as form, that even the Pollution (Figure B-7) and Land Value maps (Figure B-8) reflect the proportional design of the city. Particularly clever is the way Mr. Dodd arranged the central city into a plan that would have thrilled Le Corbusier himself. Almost the entire central city consists of high-rise residential and commercial developments surrounded by open areas of greenery. This plan allows Squaresville to have a central city that is both densely populated and valuable. It masterfully uses the rent/bid gradient (discussed in Chapter 3) to enhance the tax base. Further, the use of islands of industrial zones, rather than one or two concentrations of industrial areas, diffuses the pollution enough that it does not significantly harm the rest of the city.

Of course, I have already expressed my views on nuclear power and find myself less than impressed by the placement of power plants in the very center of the most populated areas of Symmetry City (Figure B-9). Given the parameters of the program and the possibility of accident, it would seem that those who desire to take advantage of the upside in the use of nuclear energy would want to protect the "Sims" from the downside, as well.

Mirroring Reality

Many who play SimCity like to model their own city on their favorite cities. Indeed, Will Wright admits that one rationale for including the

Rio de Janeiro flood scenario was because he liked the way the map of the city looked. Apparently, this was a motivation for some in the SimCity design contest as well. This section will discuss two such cities: the very simple Spikenard, Ohio and a simplified version of Pittsburgh, Pennsylvania.

Spikenard, Ohio

This small town (so small it isn't listed in my world atlas) was founded in 1900 by Abraham Parker (in real life) and in 1990 by S. B. Amundson (in SimLife). Located at the confluence of the Belpre and Ohio Rivers, this SimCity of 54,000 (Figure B-10) does not have any major problems. The city's budget has a positive cash flow at 5 percent taxation, severe pollution is restricted to the airport, and the city is able to support a sports stadium.

Two points are worthy of comment with regard to Spikenard, however. First, one cannot help but wonder why such a small population needs a nuclear reactor. There is plenty of room to place coal-fired plants on the outskirts of this city without causing too much pollution. Second, Mr. Amundson has employed a very useful technique to diffuse industrial pollution. He has carefully wedged industrial zones into blocks of other zones (see Figure B-11). In this way, the effects of pollution are somewhat scattered over distance.

Pittsburgh, Pennsylvania

The designer of this simulated Pittsburgh (Figure B-12), William L. Sartore, states that this map is approximately correct. This type of SimCity is fun to explore as one searches for Three Rivers Stadium and the confluence of the Monongahela, Allegheny, and Ohio rivers (Figure B-13). Beyond its relevance as a mirror image of an actual city, however, the SimMayor has utilized a clever technique to "fool" the program into increasing population density and usability of the land without taking up additional land area. A caveat must be provided before continuing with this discussion, however. Most SimCity players will consider this technique to be cheating, a method to be used as sparingly as the Funding (also known as the "Embezzling" or "Bond Issue") option described in Chapter 4.

The technique used to "fool" the SimCity program into greater population density and productivity is overlapping zones (Figure B-14). When you rezone a new zone over the top of a portion of an existing zone, the program reads the partial zone as though it were a complete zone and gives full credit for the economic, social, and political effects of the zone. Hence, you can crowd more zones into a given area than is theoretically possible.

Those who maintain that this is cheating insist that it is unfair to place zones where there is no actual room for the construction being simulated. Thus, if you cover up half of a high-rise apartment building, you can only handle half of the capacity of a high-rise apartment building. The program gives you full credit. Those who wish to rationalize their use of this technique insist that they are merely modeling multiple levels. Whereas the full zone represents an above-ground high-rise, the half-zone represents an apartment or office complex with half of its capacity underground.

Prize Winners

Because the second prize winner in Maxis Software's contest, Symmetry City, has already been mentioned, it seems appropriate to cover the first and third place winners. The third place winner was probably selected as much because of his humorous approach to the history of his city, Gilligan City, as for the design. On the other hand, the first place winner, Tjoseytown, is without a doubt a masterpiece of design.

Gilligan City

In the words of its designer, Chris Muller of Orlando, Florida, "This is what happens when Gilligan and Marianne get together on that deserted island! A pretty nice place to live, but don't look for cheap housing!" A quick look at the Land Value map (Figure B-15) will show that this is the case. Mr. Muller's exorbitant use of park space, adequate police coverage (resulting in a low crime rate), and limited number of residential zones (compared to the population) ensure high housing costs. In fact, the price of housing is the number one concern of the city's population, and it has reached crisis proportions in this city, even though everything else is relatively well taken care of.

Gilligan City would be a challenging city to continue building for any SimCity player. There is plenty of open space, but the twin points of pollution (Figure B-16) caused by mirror-image industrial areas constitute one problem that must be solved. In addition, any SimMayor will be hard-pressed to add additional housing without upsetting the carefully planned and executed park space within the city.

Tjoseytown

Greg Tjosveld, a Canadian citizen, won the 1990 design contest sponsored by Maxis Software. Mr. Tjosveld attempted to create a city with an emphasis on parkland. Looking at Figure B-17, notice how the man-made elements of the park work in conjunction with the natural elements of the park. This was accomplished with the Terrain Editor. Mr. Tjosveld built the park with the standard SimCity program. Then he saved the city. Next, he booted the Terrain Editor and loaded the city. Now he could place individual forest tiles and use the smoothing function on them. Then he saved the city and returned to the game. This created a more interesting topography for the parklands than simply relying on the grass and fountains in the SimCity game.

I am personally impressed by the high land value in the center of the city. By keeping crime (Figure B-18) and industry (Figure B-19) on the outskirts of the city, he has isolated the negative elements of urban life on the perimeter of the city and left only the positive aspects in the central city. Combining the rent/bid gradient with the bodies of water and the exorbitant quantity of parkland, this city has a remarkable concentrated land value (Figure B-20).

Lessons To Be Learned

This appendix should have demonstrated a variety of ways for you to diffuse the effects of pollution, enhance the land value of your central city, and avoid wasted space and energy. In addition, you should have learned how to "cheat" the program by overlapping zones, and you should have reviewed some of the techniques discussed with regard to the Terrain Editor in Appendix A. An understanding of how these techniques were implemented in some "expert" cities should make you a more formidable SimCity mayor.

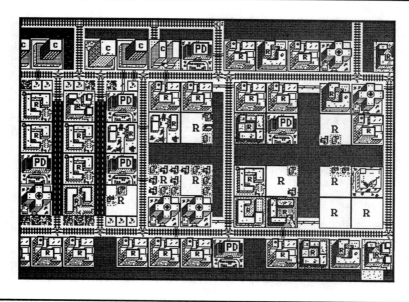

Figure B-1.　Two basic block plans in Quadripoli

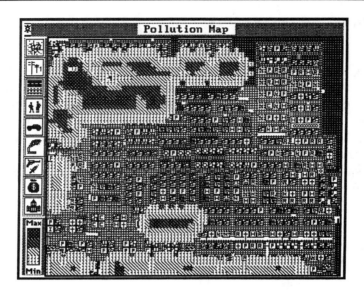

Figure B-2. Pollution in Quadripoli

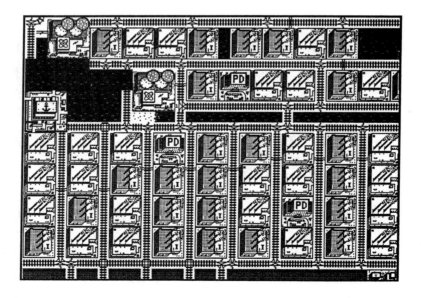

Figure B-3. Concentrated industrial area in Quadripoli

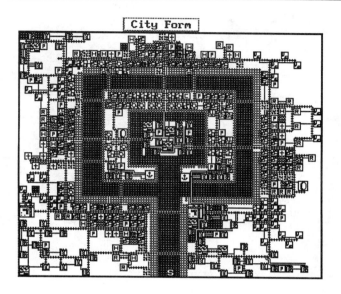

Figure B-4. Squaresville

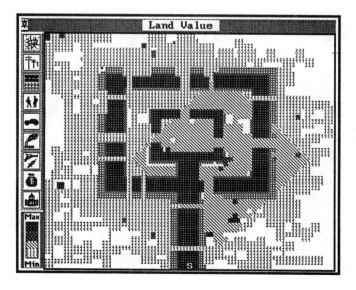

Figure B-5. Land values in Squaresville

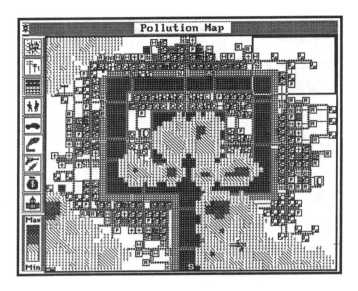

Figure B-6.   Pollution in Squaresville

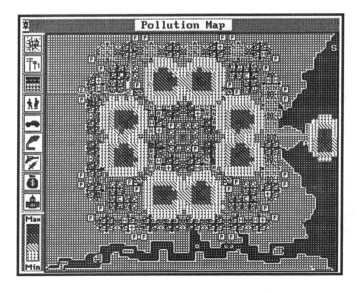

Figure B-7.   Pollution in Symmetry

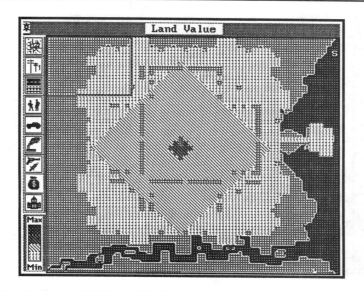

Figure B-8.   Land values in Symmetry

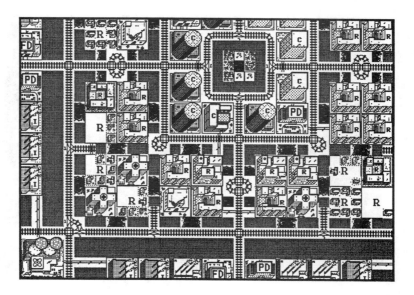

Figure B-9.   Nuclear reactors in Symmetry

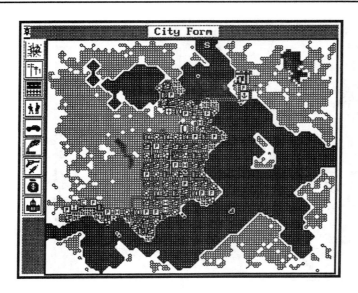

Figure B-10.   Spikenard, Ohio (SimCity style)

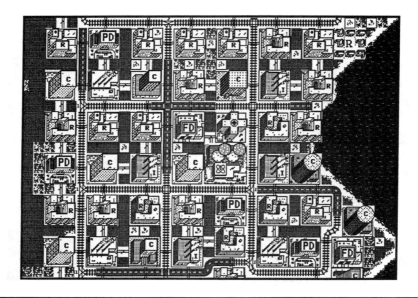

Figure B-11.   Industrial zones interspersed with other zones in Spikenard

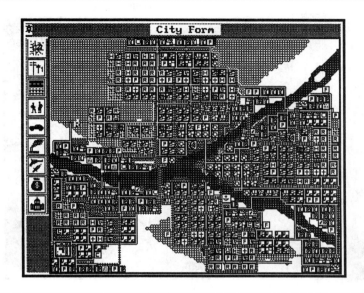

Figure B-12.   Pittsburgh, Pennsylvania (SimCity style)

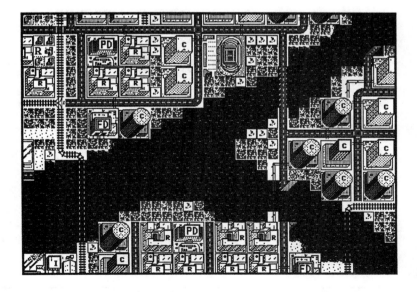

Figure B-13.   Three Rivers Stadium and environs

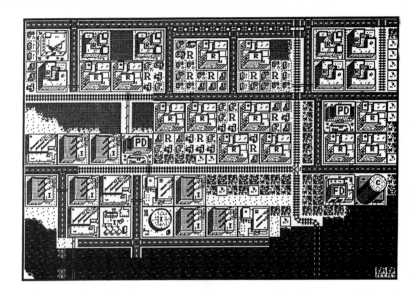

Figure B-14. Technique of overlapping zones used in Pittsburgh

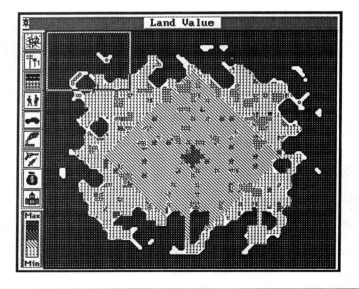

Figure B-15. Land values in Gilligan City

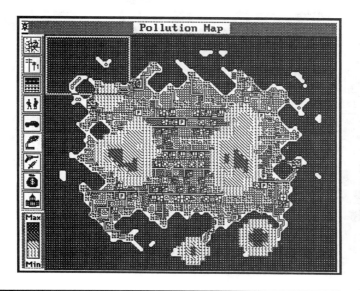

Figure B-16.   Pollution in Gilligan City

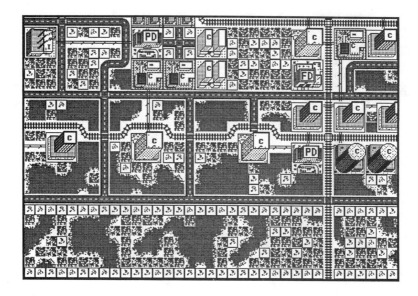

Figure B-17.   Natural forest in man-made parks in Tjoseytown

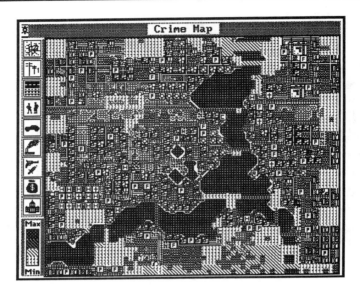

Figure B-18.   Crime in Tjoseytown

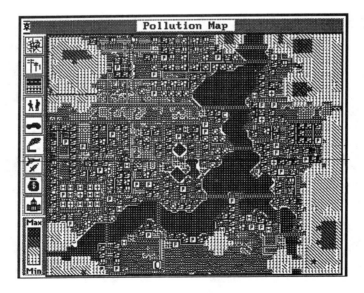

Figure B-19.   Pollution in Tjoseytown

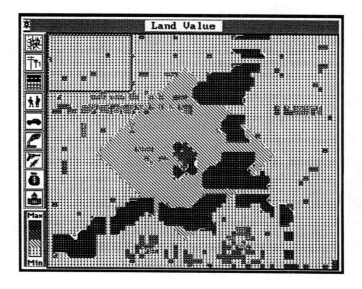

Figure B-20.   Land values in Tjoseytown

APPENDIX C
TOYS AND THE MAN: AN INTERVIEW WITH WILL WRIGHT, INVENTOR OF THE SOFTWARE TOY

Will Wright

Will Wright began work on SimCity in late 1984 or early 1985, but this was only the latest brainchild of a person with a long history of creative and innovative thought. We caught up with the man one afternoon to talk about SimCity, its prehistory, and its future. Following is the text of that conversation.

WILSON: Since you are credited with creating an entire genre of game with SimCity, namely the software toy, I was wondering what kinds of toys you grew up with.

WRIGHT: Well, chemistry sets were fun, but the problem was that they never gave you the really cool chemicals so there wasn't much that you could do with them. Fortunately, though, the neighbors had a pool and it's amazing what you can do with pool chemicals. I wouldn't want you to write anything about some of the things you can do with them. They can be pretty dangerous.

WILSON: Is there anything you can admit?

WRIGHT: I had this friend who was a tremendous chemist. He figured out how to make this chlorine-based gunpowder with a really low flash point. At one point, we almost burned my room down with it.

WILSON: Any other interesting toys?

WRIGHT: Well, I also went through the typical model building period.

WILSON: Oh, what kinds?

WRIGHT: Mostly planes, tanks, and ships. I started out with the prefab plastic ones and eventually ended up building custom ones from balsa wood. I also built dioramas, those landscapes for toy soldiers. I was particularly interested in building World War II dioramas. Actually, because of the gobs of technology they could base models on, I started getting interested in reading about the technology behind the vehicles and, at the same time, I became interested in WWII history and accelerated the learning curve.

WILSON: Did you ever play with erector sets?

WRIGHT: Actually, I did, but I soon went from erector sets to that stock aluminum you could buy at hardware stores. It was cheaper and more flexible than buying more and more erector sets. Especially when I started getting into building robots, that became my material of choice.

WILSON: How old were you when you were building these robots?

WRIGHT: By that time, I was about 16 or so.

WILSON: How did you power these robots?

WRIGHT: I used to order motors from these surplus store catalogs. At that time, the government was unloading a lot of surplus jet aircraft and you could get these great DC motors that were about 400Hz and sold for twenty to thirty dollars, even though they had originally cost the government several hundred dollars each. Oh, I also found that cordless drills were a great source of motors. You could get four or five amp motors with incredible torque from cordless drills.

WILSON: So, what brought you from chlorine gunpowder and electric robots to computers?

WRIGHT: It was the robots that actually got me into computers. After all, you have to have controllers to make robots really work and I needed the computer knowledge to make the controllers work. One robot I built had a combination walkie-talkie and modem that I fixed up to work as a wireless modem-link. That let me control this robot by remote control. When I was 18 or 19 years old, I used an Apple II to interface with a robot that I'd equipped with a Polaroid range finder. It was pretty interesting because it could actually map the room.

Later, I tried putting one of those little Timex Sinclair computers onboard the robot, but I couldn't ever get it to be stable. Since it used the same grounding as the robot's motor, it would reset the computer every time the motor turned on.

WILSON: Did you enroll in courses on computer programming in order to learn how to program or were you self-taught?

WRIGHT: Most of my computer knowledge was self-taught, but I did take a few courses in computer programming. Most of them were taken in New York City in a place called the New School for Social Research. It was located right next to NYU.

WILSON: How did you end up there?

WRIGHT: I had been in school in Louisiana for a few years, but the structured university approach didn't agree with me very much. I would keep getting excited about certain areas of knowledge, but the professors were always assigning other things. On my own, I read some articles by Mark Chartrand and discovered that he was teaching courses in the commercialization of space. The whole concept sounded very interesting to me. So, when it turned out that these courses were in New York and being taught at this school, I moved to New York and got an apartment there. At the same time as I was taking Chartrand's courses, I was taking a lot of programming courses.

New York City was great. They had great surplus stores downtown and I would go down every day and rummage through the things. I'd buy all kinds of stuff and bring it back to create more robots.

WILSON: Since you mentioned your course work in the commercialization of space, I can't help but wonder if your robotics interest was geared toward robots in the home or in space exploration?

WRIGHT: I was always interested in the home robot. There were so many interesting things they could do. Unfortunately, they didn't do much good if you had to have a human being there controlling them, so there needed to be a program behind them that could free up the human being. It didn't take long before I realized that it wasn't the hardware, but the software which was the real challenge. As soon as I came to that realization, my incentive to build robots lessened and my incentive to create software increased.

WILSON: So, how did you end up moving from the idea of creating software in general to creating games?

WRIGHT: At age 21, I moved to California to be with Joell, the woman who was to become my wife. I was playing a lot of computer games at the time, like FS1 Flight Simulator and Computer Ambush. Since I was getting totally into software, I decided to do a computer game to support myself and get more familiar with AI and assembly language. The Commodore 64 had just been announced at that point and I decided to learn on that platform in order to exploit the window of opportunity. I started playing around with ideas and Raid On Bungling Bay came out of that.

WILSON: So, the economics caused you to change from an Apple II to a Commodore 64 programmer?

WRIGHT: Not really. I was using the Apple II as my development system. Since the Apple had been around for so many years, there were much better programming tools available on it. I simply wrote a patch so that everything I compiled could be converted at the push of a button. I never actually wrote anything *on* the C-64. Frankly, it was my desire to avoid the Commodore disk drive entirely.

WILSON: I can't help but wonder if the original SimCity was developed for the Commodore in the same way?

WRIGHT: The original Commodore version was, but I wrote new code for the Macintosh version.

WILSON: About how old were you when you wrote Raid on Bungling Bay?

WRIGHT: I was 22 at the time. Of course, by the time I was getting near the end of the project, I had built an editor in order to create terrain tiles for the cities which were to be bombed in the game. By the end of the project, I discovered that I was having a lot of fun playing with the editor, more fun than blowing up the islands. I kept playing with it, even after the game was done. In fact, it was a lot like building the little dioramas in my youth.

WILSON: So, was it the science fiction story by Stanislaw Lem about Trurl the constructor or playing with the terrain tiles that actually inspired SimCity? I think you said I messed up the chronology in the introduction of the previous edition of this book.

WRIGHT: I think I had actually read *The Cyberiad*, the collection with the Trurl story, years before, but I reread it about the period I was playing with the terrain tiles. It was just enough to give me the strange idea that I ought to try to make them come to life.

WILSON: Then, how far along was SimCity when your neighbor got involved?

WRIGHT: It was fairly far along when I showed it to him. Bruce Joffe is an actual urban planner and he got all excited about it. Since he had studied under Jay Forester at M.I.T., he was able to slip me a lot of books on urban dynamics.

WILSON: What was the hardest part of creating the game?

WRIGHT: I don't think it was developing any particular model. The hardest part was balancing the different models together. We had a crime model, traffic model, power model, economic model, population model and so forth. The challenge was to juggle the resolution of each individual calculation so that they fit together correctly and were measured in a synchronized time pattern.

WILSON: What do you consider your most elegant design solution?

WRIGHT: There were a lot of things in there where I would start out with an algorithm that was okay, but then I would keep coming up with ways to improve it. In particular, I had to spend a lot of time on the power model and the traffic model.

One decision I made early on that I was really happy with was the economic-based system in which land value was central to the way everything integrated together. It made the overall model less stable, more dynamic and hence, more realistic. Some people call it "Life on the edge of chaos." I thought it was very effective.

WILSON: Were you surprised at how much SimCity has been put to serious uses? After all, it's been used in college courses and by real planners. That isn't exactly what you expect from a game.

WRIGHT: I was surprised at all the uses for it, but as I was researching it, I was sort of surprised that no one had done it before. I had seen extremely detailed traffic models, housing value models and population/demographic models, but I had never seen anything that really tied them all together. I guess that makes sense. They were having a hard enough time getting the separate models to work that they weren't ready to create a comprehensive overview. The same thing was true in my SimEarth research, as well.

What I discoverd was that a lot of urban experts are so specialized that they have created walls in their heads. For example, there are power experts who don't know anything about water and don't want to know. There are traffic experts who don't know anything about power and don't care to know. The truly amazing part of SimCity is the comprehensive way everything pulls together and relates to other facets of the model.

WILSON: Speaking of real-life uses for SimCity, your company has set up a special division to create simulation systems related to reality-based models. Do you consult with Maxis on any of these special projects like the SimRefinery you were creating for Chevron?

WRIGHT: I work at the design level on some of these special projects. I usually talk to the designers and give them some pointers for approaching certain types of algorithms. I don't usually work on the coding level unless I can give them some piece of programming from SimCity or SimEarth that might model something they need in a SimRefinery.

WILSON: Is there a lot of demand for these special projects?

WRIGHT: I would rather say that *interest* in these vertical projects is extremely high. I don't consider it demand until people are willing to plop down the appropriate amount of money. It remains to be seen what the demand actually is. Of course, the demand is tied to what we can actually do.

WILSON: Getting back to the game itself, is there any advice you could offer to beginning players?

WRIGHT: When I play it, it is all land value, land value, land value. It's just like the old real estate cliché where there are three rules to success: location, location, location. SimCity is very much a spatial game. Just as in chess, both sides may have the same pieces on the board, but the bottom line is how they lay out. You could have two cities with the same number of identical zones and terrain, but it is the way it is laid out that counts. It's a living jigsaw puzzle. I think it's really interesting to note how they relate to each other. Of course, when I say land value, I'm talking about creating positive cash flow and covering the expense of your infrastructure. That's the way most people play the game.

Now, I also like to pick a spot on the map and use my imagination to put myself on the street corner and try to figure out what it looks and feels like. I try to imagine what different spots in the city feel like. I pick out my favorite spots and then try to figure out what I like about them and why.

WILSON: Is that where you got the idea for putting customized signposts in SimCity 2000?

WRIGHT: I actually got the idea for the signposts from some research by Kevin Lynch. His research shows that people map cities mentally by creating certain landmarks. The sign idea in SimCity 2000 reflects this mental mapping. Some are famous landmarks, but some are personal landmarks. The other interesting fact is that distances shorten in one's mind as we become familiar with the routes we regularly take. I wanted to be able create a mental map in the players' minds that would personalize the maps. It makes a much bigger impact to say that there is a fire in Brooklyn Heights than it does to say there's a fire in the upper right-hand corner of the map.

WILSON: Speaking of the new game, why did you return to Sim-City when your company is successful enough that you can do anything you want?

WRIGHT: Well, the good part about writing SimCity 2000 is that I'm getting to add all this stuff that I really wanted to add to the game and that people wanted me to add. But the truth is that I have a dream project that I really want to work on, though I can't tell you much more about it other than that it is going to be a very personal game for everyone. It will offer more because it will get people into more than just design.

WILSON: So, what have you discovered?

WRIGHT: I discovered that there is this entire discipline of abstract design theory. This is a fascinating study of the eras of design.

There are times when architects have emphasized iterative design (incremental design with add-on functions and ornamentation) versus the simulated annealing approach (a computer optimization term for creating the most efficient link between nodes). I'm really impressed with the latter. It's a top-down approach where design is derived from activities and functional relationships. Then, the architect groups those activities together and creates transportation corridors. It's pretty impressive. I use some of the same techniques in software design, but these guys are way ahead of me. Anyway, that's my next project.

BIBLIOGRAPHY

Adcock, F. E. 1960. *The Roman Art of War Under the Republic.* New York: Barnes & Noble, Inc.

Bender, Thomas. 1982. "The American City: What shaped its development?" In *Cities: The Forces that Shape Them,* Lisa Taylor, ed. Washington, DC: The Smithsonian Institution 50-53.

Briggs, David. 1974. "Transport." In *Encyclopedia of Urban Planning,* Arnold Whittick, ed. New York: McGraw-Hill Book Co.

Gallion, Arthur B. and Simon Eisner. 1986. *The Urban Pattern: City Planning and Design.* New York: Van Nostrand Reinhold Co.

Gleick, James. 1987. *Chaos: Making A New Science.* New York: Penguin Books.

Godschalk, David R., David J. Brower, and Timothy Beatley. 1989. *Catastrophic Coastal Storms: Hazard Mitigation and Development Management.* Durham, NC: Duke University Press.

Greenberg, Michael, Donald A. Krueckeberg, and Connie Michaelson. 1978. *Local Population and Employment Projection Techniques.* New Brunswick, NJ: Center for Urban Policy Research.

Jacobs, Jane. 1961. *The Death and Life of Great American Cities.* New York: Random House.

_____. 1969. *The Economy of Cities.* New York: Doubleday & Co.

King, John. 1989. "In the Wake of the Quake." *Planning.* Dec:12-17.

Koester, Frank. 1914. *Modern City Planning and Maintenance.* New York: McBride, Nast and Co.

Le Corbusier. 1987. *The City of To-Morrow and Its Planning.* New York: Dover Publications, Inc.

Myers, Norman (ed.). 1984. *Gaia: An Atlas of Planet Management.* New York: Doubleday & Co.

Nakicenovic, Nebojsa. 1988. "Dynamics and Replacement of U.S. Transport Infrastructures." In *Cities and Their Vital Systems: Infrastructure Past, Present, and Future,* Jesse H. Ausubel and Robert Herman, eds. Washington, DC: National Academy Press 175-221.

Parker, Horace. 1967. "The Historic Valley of Temecula: Thriving, Tempting Temecula of 1909." Balboa Island, CA: Paisano Press.

Pournelle, Jerry. 1990. "Optical Disk Daze." *Byte.* Feb:99-114.

Speiregen, Paul D. (ed.). 1968. *On the Art of Designing Cities: Selected Essays of Elbert Peets.* Cambridge, MA: Massachusetts Institute of Technology Press.

Svenson, Arthur G. 1984. *Earthquakes, Earth Scientists, and Seismic-Safety Planning in California.* Lanham, MD: University Press of America.

Toffler, Alvin. 1980. *The Third Wave.* New York: Bantam Doubleday.

Vance, James E. 1982. "The American Urban Geography: The old world strongly influenced the new." In *Cities: The Forces that Shape Them,* Lisa Taylor, ed. Washington, DC: Smithsonian Institution 53-54.

INDEX

A

Air quality, 84-88
Airplane crashes, 110
Airports, 140-142
Airports icon, 26-27
"The American City: What shaped its development?", 48, 185
Amiga, SimCity on, 4-5, 8
Amundson, S.B., 170
Aosta (Italy), ground plan, 42
Archaeological sites in Temecula, 116
Aristotle, 40
Atari ST, SimCity on, 5
Atlas of SimCity competition cities, 167-183

B

Bad News City simulation, 156-157
Bauhaus commune, 3
Bender, Thomas, 48, 185
Bern scenario
    bottlenecks, 71-72
    light rail to straighten bottlenecks, 73
    satellite development for, 78
    useless roads on the west side, 79
Bibliography, 185-187
Big City simulation, 156-158
Bond issues, 80
Boston 2010 scenario, 91-93
Bottlenecks, traffic, 70-72

Bulldozer icon, 9, 11-12

C

C-64/128. *See* Commodore 64/128
Chaos: Making a New Science, 129, 185
Cheating with Terrain Editor, 154, 170-171, 173
Checkerboards, 17
City Form map, 31-33
The City of To-Morrow and Its Planning, 69, 186
City Services map, 34
Cohorts, 56
Cohort-survival chart, 57
Colonial Williamsburg, sketch of, 46
Commercial considerations, 60-61
Commercial zones
    growth factors for, 21
    internal market share, 60
    radius of influence, 60
Commercial Zones icon, 20
Continuous expansion (as development type), 47
Curved grids, 72
Commodore 64/128, SimCity on, 5-6, 9

D

Deadwood City simulation, 158-160
The Death and Life of Great American Cities, 68, 76, 186
Design errors, 139-147
Detroit, history of, 48-49

Detroit scenario
  crime concentrations, 88-89
  Fiscal Budget window, 87
  pollution concentrations, 88
Disasters, 95-110
Disasters menu, 37-38
Dodd, Jon, 169

E

Early cities, 40-46
Earthquakes, 98-107
  liquefaction, 101
  San Francisco scenario, 102-107
  seismic engineering, 99
Ecology and entropy, 83-93
The Economy of Cities, 48, 186
Eisner, Simon, 68, 185
Electrical demand, 124-125
Embezzling function, 80
Endangered species, 118
Entropy
  and ecology, 83-93
  versus Gaia hypothesis, 130-132
  and nurture, 136
Estimated migration rate, 56
Evaluation graphs, 10- and 120-year, 35
Evaluation window, 30-31
Export multiplier effect, 60
Exurbia phenomenon, 53

F

Feedback mechanisms, 133-136
Finigan City simulation, 158, 160
Fire breaks, 17
Fire departments, 140-142
Fire Departments icon, 24
Fire Protection map, 105, 108
Fiscal Budget window, 34, 36, 87
Flood plain development, 96-98
Forester, Dr. Jay, xxiii
Fort Worth (Texas), 85-86
Fredsville simulation, 161

G

Gaia hypothesis, 129-137
Gallion, Arthur B., 68, 185
Geometric cities, 167-169
Geometrical grid, 42
Gilligan City simulation, 171-172, 180-181
Gleick, James, 129, 185
Greenbelt, 45
Greendale (Wisconsin), 51-52
Grid patterns in American urban develop-
  ment, 49-50
Gridiron plan, 40
Gropius, Walter, 3
Gruen plan (Fort Worth, Texas), 85-86

H

Hamburg (Germany) scenario, 107, 109
  electrical demand, 125
  Fire Protection map, 108
Happy, IL simulation, 161-162
Haussmannization, 69-72
Haussmann, Baron Georges-Eugene, 69
Hill, Walter, 168
Hippodamus, 40
"The Historic Valley of Temecula", 112,
  186
Hospitals, 119-121
Human resources and problems, 55-64

I

IBM, SimCity on, 6-8
Icons, 9
  Airports, 26-27
  Bulldozer, 9, 11-12
  Commercial Zones, 20
  Fire Departments, 24
  identified, 11
  Industrial Zones, 22
  Maps window, 33
  Parks, 15-16
  Police Departments, 22, 24
  Population Maps, 34

Icons, *continued*
    Power Lines, 14
    Power Plants, 25-26
    Residential Zones, 16, 18-19
    Roads, 13-14
    Sea Ports, 26
    Stadiums, 24-25
    Transit Lines, 15
Import replacing multiplier effect, 60
Industrial considerations, 61-62
Industrial satellite cities, 51
Industrial zones, negative factors surrounding, 23
Industrial Zones icon, 22
Intercept strategy, 144
Island function (Terrain Editor), 153
Isotropic transport plane, 59

J

Jacobs, Jane, 48, 68, 76, 186
Joffe, Bruce, xxiii-xxiv
Joffeberg simulation, 163

K

Karlsruhe (Germany), 43
    ground plan, 44
Key to the City, 75-76
Koester, Frank, 51, 186

L

Land rent (for motor vehicles), 68
Land use, and traffic planning, 75-80
Land value, managing, 57-62
Le Corbusier, 46, 69, 186
Light rail
    avoiding derailing, 142-143
    in Bern scenario, 73
    problems with, 76-77
Linear City simulation, 163-164
London, 42-43

M

Macintosh, SimCity on, 7-8
Mader, George, 101

Manufacturing center, 60
Maps, types of
    City Form, 31-33
    City Services, 34
    Crime Rate, 34, 131
    Fire Protection, 34, 105, 108
    Police Protection, 34
    Pollution, 34, 84-85
    Power Grid, 106
Maps window, 31-32
    icons, 33
Medieval City simulation, 164-165
Meltdown (Boston scenario), 91-93
Message bar, 9
Migration rate, estimated, 56
Miletus (Asia Minor), ground plan, 41
Modern City Planning and Maintenance, 51, 186
Monster Attack scenario (Tokyo), 109
Motor vehicles, versus transportation animals, 67
Muller, Chris, 171

N

Nakicenovic, Nebojsa, 66, 186
Needs gap equation, 28
Nintendo, SimCity on, 7
Nuclear power issues, 89-93
Nucleated expansion, 51
Nurture
    as the antithesis of entropy, 136
    as natural, 129-137

O

Open spaces in urban planning, 51-53

P

Paleontologically significant sites in Temecula, 117
Paris, 69-70
Parker, Horace, 112, 186
Parking problems, 63

Parks and recreation, 123-124
Parks icon, 15-16
PERT (Program Evaluation and Review
   Technique), 29-36
Pittsburgh (Pennsylvania) simulation,
   170-171, 179-180
Planning mistakes, avoiding, 139-143
Planning successes, examples of, 143-144,
   167-183
Police departments, 63
Police Departments icon, 22, 24
Pollution map, 34, 84-85
Population bomb, 55
Population density, 62-64
Population growth
   cohort-survival method, 56-57
   estimated migration rate, 56
   projections, 56-57
   residual method, 56
   vital rates, 56
Population Maps icon, 34
Ports, in American urban history, 47-49
Power Grid map, 106
Power Lines icon, 14
Power Plants icon, 25-26
Protecting sensitive and irreplaceable
   resources, 114-118

Q

Quadripoli simulation, 167-168, 173-174

R

Rail lines. *See* Light rail
Random terrain generator, 151-152
Recreation and parks, 123-124
Redevelopment, 63
Rent/bid gradient, 58
Residential Zones icon, 16, 18-19
Resources, protecting irreplaceable,
   114-118
Rio de Janeiro scenario
   after the flood, 99
   before the flood, 98
   flood prevention, 96-97
   open space in southwest, 100

Roadless city, 76-77
Roads
   ingress and egress, 139-140
   patterns of, 13
   relationship with growth, 66
Roads icon, 13-14
Roosth, Joe, 167

S

Salisbury, Harrison, 68
San Francisco scenario, 102-107
   after the 1906 quake, 103
   before the 1906 quake, 102
   fire from the quake, 103-104
   Fire Protection radius map, 105
   Power Grid map after the quake, 106
Sartore, William L., 170
Satellite cities, 51
Satellite development, 77-80
School districts, 121-122
Sea Ports icon, 26
Seashore development, 96-98
Seismic engineering, 99
Seismic zoning, 101
SimCity
   basic screen, 10
   getting started, 4-7
   history of, xxiii-xxiv
   main title screen, 5
Simecula scenario, 125-127
Simulating city services, 119-125
Smoothing function (Terrain Editor), 153,
   155
Speculator's towns, 49
Spikenard, Ohio simulation, 170, 178
Squaresville simulation, 168-169, 175-176
Stadiums icon, 24-25
Standard town plat, 49-50
Symmetry City simulation, 169, 176-177

T

Tampa Bay (Florida) scenario, 145-147

Temecula Valley (Southern California), 111-127
    archaeological sites in, 116
    electrical demand, 124-125
    endangered species of, 118
    history of, 112, 114
    hospital placement, 119-121
    location of, 113
    paleontological sites in, 117
    parks and recreation, 123-124
    power substations, 126
    school districts, 121-122
    waste management, 122, 123
Terrain Editor, 149-165
    cheating with, 154, 170-171, 173
    editing tools, 155-156
    installing the disks, 150-152
    island function, 153
    modified random terrain generator, 151
    nine city simulations, 156-165
    smoothing function, 153, 155
    System menu, 152
    Terrain menu, 152-153
    tile-by-tile terrain generator, 151-152
Terrain tiles, 15
The Third Wave, 55, 187
Tile-by-tile terrain generator, 151-152
Tjoseytown simulation, 172, 182-183

Tjosveld, Greg, 172
Toffler, Alvin, 55, 187
Tokyo scenario, 109
Traffic calculations, 72-75
Traffic congestion, 65-81
Traffic planning, and land use, 75-80
Transit Lines icon, 15
Transportation alternatives, 41

U

The Urban Pattern: City Planning and Design, 68, 185
Urban planning
    history of, 39-53
    purpose of, 27-29

V

Victory screen for SimCity scenarios, 76

W

Washington D.C., L'Enfant's plan, 44-45
Waste management, 122-123
Windows menu, 29-30
Wright, Will, xxiii-xxiv, 65

Z

Zoning, 51, 101